HEINRICH HEINE WHEN A STUDENT AT GÖTTINGEN.

From a drawing by a college mate.

THE FAMILY LIFE

OF

HEINRICH HEINE

THE FAMILY LIFE

OF

HEINRICH HEINE

One Hundred and Twenty-two Family Letters
of the Poet hitherto unpublished
from his College Days
to his Death

BY HIS NEPHEW

BARON LUDWIG VON EMBDEN

FROM THE GERMAN BY

CHARLES DE KAY

WITH FOUR PORTRAITS

HASKELL HOUSE PUBLISHERS LTD.

Publishers of Scarce Scholarly Books

NEW YORK, N. Y. 10012

1970

First Published 1892

HASKELL HOUSE PUBLISHERS Ltd.
Publishers of Scarce Scholarly Books
280 LAFAYETTE STREET
NEW YORK, N. Y. 10012

Library of Congress Catalog Card Number: 76-133280

Standard Book Number 8383-1179-2

Printed in the United States of America

PREFACE TO THE ENGLISH TRANSLATION.

THE first collection of the works of Heinrich Heine in seven volumes was published in America in 1865, closely followed by the complete works in twenty volumes issued by Messrs. Hoffman & Campe of Hamburg. As early as 1855 a translation of the "Reisebilder" by Charles G. Leland appeared in Philadelphia, and in 1864 the "Buch der Lieder." A selection of his songs and ballads translated by Emma Lazarus, a poetess whose end was in some respects like that of the Jewish poet, appeared in New York in 1881, and another selection translated by Frances Helman has just made its appearance. It is therefore likely that a translation of the familiar letters of Heine addressed chiefly to his mother and sister will find readers on this side of the Atlantic.

It would be indeed strange if so modern a thinker and one who in some respects stands with the first in German literature should fail to remain a figure of uncommon picturesqueness and to challenge the interest of those who regard as antiquated his views of the struggle between the people and the privileged classes. It is not only as a literary star of the first brightness, but as captain in the battle America has been fighting for more than one century, that Heine claims our sympathies.

The letters are not literary at all. Always a foe to fine writing in his letters home, Heine was often loose in construction and sometimes ungrammatical, but at the same time his German is racy. They reflect the hopes and needs of the man, his attitude of mind toward money, his wife, household, publishers, friends, enemies and relatives. They are Heine in his well moments seated beneath his vine, making sly fun of Mathilde and Cocotte the parrot, or Heine on his invalid's chair, spluttering fiercely against a brother who has blundered while negotiating with old Campe the publisher. Broad wit is not absent, a sort of wit that recalls Rabelais rather than Sterne; but the editor of these letters has suppressed more than he has allowed to stand. Heine was often the victim of slanderers of the true Germanic sort who invented and garbled with a heavy hand. The letters permit us to light up many an obscure corner and at least approach a separation of fantastic matter from facts in Heine's essays in autobiography. Here and there are keen thrusts like those which have endeared him to people who can laugh when a hand which is light on the sword-grasp pierces a dullard; but now and then the same hand is caught swinging a club or hurling a stone, for all the world like a naughty boy in the street.

In presenting us with the "eternal womanly" Goethe served the world well, but he failed to leave us an equivalent phrase for the "eternal Jewish," a question that is always with us. At a moment when that cheerful practice of the middle ages, Jew-baiting, seems revived in Germany, these letters are not inopportune. Nations that call themselves Teutonic make much of home-love and of the constancy of the domestic affections among themselves, which

they credit to race; it is therefore well in
the case of so conspicuous a genius as Heine
to note that his intimate life is a witness to the
repute of Jews as husbands, fathers, uncles, sons.
It may be that the domestic virtues so clearly
and naturally shown in them will do something
to disarm the wrath oi people who may have
good reason to deplore the result of some con-
test between Aryan and Semitic wits.

Yet certain foibles which are so common in
Jews that they may be called racial are not want-
ing. While striving to gain two chief ends, the
certainty of a sufficient pension to allow him to
live in Paris, and, later, a support for his wife
after his death, he shows in these letters the
suppleness, the tendency to quick temper and
the readiness for ruthless revenge which many
Jews exhibit to-day and for which the Bible is
one long precedent.

If it were not so sad it were almost comical to
trace here the methods Heine used in order to
bring pressure to bear on his rich uncle Salomon
Heine and on that uncle's heir through the
poet's mother and sister living in Hamburg; his
way of forcing the publisher to better terms, and

his ill-concealed threats to publish what his cousins wished suppressed. There is something ghoulish in Heine hoarding an assortment of family skeletons, to rattle them now and then and so keep his well-to-do relatives alive to the fact that he was not dead yet.

But against this slipperiness of the poet his love of mother and sister shine all the brighter. There is no underthought here; here no wires are pulled. The fascination which his genius and sorrowful later life have always exercised is not lessened when we find him striving by an elaborate edifice of lies and mystifications to keep his old mother ignorant of his frightful condition, and then, as soon as he is sufficiently at ease to afford it, presenting sister and nieces with Paris gowns.

Many things that Aryans attribute to the Jews are not at all racial, but merely common to humanity. It does seem, however, that the peculiar mixture of generosity and meanness reflected from Heine's character in these letters is typical of the race. While poor he was forever wailing over his wife's extravagance (my squanderer was the constant nickname he gave

her) yet he adored her, was only happy when
she was near, labored for her alone and as soon
as he had a fair income gave fine gifts to
those he loved.

His will, translated from the French in
the appendix, contains a statement of the
chief object of his life. This was to work for
a removal of the barriers of prejudice between
France and Germany, which had been strengthened by the Napoleonic wars and in nowise
weakened by subsequent events.

That this was not an idea which grew up during his illness appears from the short sketch of
his life which Heine sent to Philarète Chasles
in 1835 :

"So far as concerns the Teutomaniacs, those
German old women, whose patriotism consists
merely in a blind hatred of France, I have pur-
sued them with acrimony in all my writings.
This is an animosity which dates from the time
of the college fraternity (*Burschenshaft*) to which
I belonged."

Indeed Heine of Düsseldorf as a boy was for
many years under the French flag; he had only
the most delightful memories of the French oc-

cupation and he always admired Napoleon the
Great. In this he was by no means alone among
Germans. Here we find him using French
words and phrases and have his own evi-
dence to prove that success in France founded
his literary and financial success in Germany.
Therefore he was well prepared for the task of
reconciling the French and Germans, better prepared than Matthew Arnold was at a later date
when he tried to soften the rooted dislike of
the Briton for the Frank.

Germans, however, never forgave Heine for the
ridicule he cast on them, for the atrocious and
often true things he said of them as they were
in the earlier half of the present century. The
monument in his memory planned for Düsseldorf
was not built, although the Empress of Austria, a
member of that royal family of Bavaria which
he had so virulently lampooned in the person
of Ludwig I, was an active patroness of the
movement.

Mr. von Embden, to whom we owe these letters
in their present shape, speaks of the unification
of Germany as if Heine would have applauded it.
But surely no man would have stood more aghast

at a result which puts his hated Prussians in command, continues the existence of kings, princelets and *Junkerthum*, justifies the insolence of professional soldiers and has carried to an extraordinary degree the old tension between Frenchmen and Germans.

Indeed, as we see it now, not the least tragic part of Heine's life is the failure of his work in this regard. But idolized Goethe could not have accomplished that task, much less one whose calm was anything but Olympian, whose pen dropped gall, who was a member of an envied and detested race and whose residence in France gave apparent countenance to charges of cowardice and want of patriotism.

Heine had his own courage and his own patriotism; they were not of a very lofty kind, but are shown in his satires on the Germans. His impish wit, his quick turns to escape the cudgel wielded by the Deutscher Michel are amusing; but to the Michael of Germany it must have seemed that they were meant, not so much to reform him as to amuse his old enemies, the "Franz-hosen," as, with a play upon their supposed love of personal adornment, Michael of Germany loves to call the French.

The mention of Matthew Arnold will suffice to recall his Essays in Criticism and the appreciation he showed of Heine's work in life. He calls the " Romanzero " " a collection of poems written in the first years of his illness with his whole power and charm still in them." But Heine himself, we know now, considered it inferior work produced after his powers had been weakened. Writing to his mother in December 1851 he says: " I assure you it is a very weak book—but nobody must say so. I wrote it with my powers broken." Had Matthew Arnold written his essay after the publication of Carlyle's diary, he would have found a parallel between these two singular spirits, their railing, and their unhappy later lives, but also much to serve as contrast; for Heine was at once poet and clear thinker up to a certain point, while Carlyle was a prose master whose brain was far from clear. Both had points of resemblance in external matters and both attacked humbugs to the best of their ability. But it may be said that of the two it was Heine

who seems to have had a suspicion that he
himself was at times more or less of a hum-
bug. He took himself less seriously than
Carlyle.

When we would grapple with the secret of
his genius, however, Heine proves evasive. We
see him studying English literature, translating
Byron, popularizing the chief men and women in
Shakspere's plays and catching a distinct whiff of
the manner of Lawrence Sterne in his prose. He
calls Sterne somewhere the born equal of Shakspere. We then see him exploring Spanish
literature and repeating in German the simple
lilt of the old Spanish ballads. But his real
attraction does not lie in the colors which he
took on so easily and used for his own purpose
with so much *naïveté* and skill. It was not his
criticism of pictures or books or philosophy that
made people care for his work; it was the
peculiar quality of the *Weltschmerz* that rose from
his verse and prose—sweet, but with a suggestion of death, like jasmine flowers too long imprisoned in their box. It is this taint which set
Heine apart from other writers and makes him
so much relished by thousands who possibly

may be at a loss to understand the origin of their pleasure.

It is true that Heine was not a well man even when young; we perceive that from the letters now published written while at the universities.

He wrote to Philarète Chasles in 1835: " My studies, interrupted by romantic moods, by endeavors to establish myself, by love and by other sicknesses were continued from 1819 on at Bonn, at Göttingen and at Berlin. I lived four years and a half in Berlin where I was in friendly relations with the most remarkable men of learning and where I was afflicted with a dagger stroke in the loins given me by a certain Scheller from Dantzic—whose name I shall never forget, because he is the only man who has understood how to wound me in the most poignant fashion."

But the peculiar flavor which is his final charm does not spring from his health, though bad health may have assisted it. Nor can we suppose that his love affair in extreme youth with a cousin in Hamburg was the moving cause. We must look to the race of which he is so brilliant an ornament for an explanation that is adequate.

Heine was neither a German nor a Frenchman, least of all a Greek as he fondly imagined himself; he was a Jew. As such he occupied that position apart which all the European peoples feel the Jews to occupy and which some people openly resent. It is only in this way that the extraordinary phenomena of the present day can be explained—Jews detested, feared and persecuted in Russia, Jews detested still and feared in Germany, Jews envied if not so generally detested in France. It is unchristian and wrong; it is cowardly if you will, but this attitude of large numbers of men in Europe is a fact and a force which were far better acknowledged and faced than explained away by half statements. It was this feeling toward the Jews, then and now unaccountably violent in Germany, it was this feeling acting on his sensitive nerves that gave its peculiar flavor to the *Weltschmerz* one tastes in Heine's works.

The Jews are a profoundly uncomfortable people who, as a race—and Heine often pointed it out—are far removed from the serenity of the Greeks of the classic period. Circumstances having to do with their past as well as the present

force them to seek the towns; only when
necessity compels are they dwellers in country
parts. Their nimble wits give them a distinct
advantage in crowds; but it may be noted that
in the most favorable circumstances they are the
greatest grumblers on earth; nothing pleases them,
or if something should, their keen wit sees some
advantage in pretending they are dissatisfied.
This is the chief reason, and probably the only
reason, for the attempts made in America to ex-
clude Jews from certain hotels. The keepers of
hotels, used to the long-suffering, abused Christian of our stripe, cannot put up with people who
are just the opposite, who are eternally growling
and grumbling at prices, the quality of food and
service, and are ever looking for their rights. As
if our public had any rights!

One of the words that occur most frequently
in Heine's familiar letters is *verdriesslich*. He
is always out of patience with little things.
Yet—like his race again—he suffered real agony
and years of agony with a constancy and pluck
that were simply heroic.

Heine has in his published works a strong
feminine element. His letters to the family in

Hamburg show the trait even more; many sound like the hasty scrawl of a young girl from her boarding school. But this is not saying that he was unmanly; it is merely trying to define the man by bringing a certain trait into relief.

Heine had many bitter quarrels in his life with members of his family and others, but the bitterest was with another Jew, Ludwig Börne. The chapters of his book on Börne are among the happiest, funniest and most ruthless, nor are Jews by any means the last to enjoy the fun he had at their expense. It was a Jew with whom he fought that duel which was the cause of his marrying, just before the affair, the young French woman with whom he had been living after the fashion of the Quartier Latin. As with his baptism, so with his marriage: the laws of the Christians forced him to give up a Pagan wedlock— or shall we say an Oriental?—and accept the Christian forms.

His self-centered character, rarely given to admiring other writers who were contemporaries, appears in a negative way. Though it is certain he knew Béranger, La Fayette, Victor Hugo,

George Sand, Théophile Gautier and the elder
Dumas, we look in vain through these letters
for a mention of them. Often one is ready to
accuse him of selfish neglect of those at home, so
devoid are his letters of descriptions and anec-
dotes which, had he taken the trouble to give
them, would have proved a godsend to the Hamburg home. No ; early in life after graduation
he seems to have written himself out in that
sort of correspondence ; at least we may give
him the benefit of the doubt and suppose that
the letters home which were burned in Hamburg's conflagration were of this kind. Later,
of course, when a confirmed invalid, it is perfectly natural that he should have little leisure
and indeed little eyesight to amuse his old
mother and his sister.

After reading these letters and the comments
of his nephew, sister, brother and niece which
have been added here and there, one finds that
Heine remains as before a man without a country, a partisan rejected of all political parties,
who was not even in the domain of religion
either a Christian or Jew or philosopher, and
whose one effort to benefit mankind increased

rather than lessened the national hatred it sought to remove.

But then he was a very wonderful poet. Why ask for more?

CHARLES DE KAY.

NEW YORK, *January* 1, 1893.

Footnotes added by the translator are marked TR., and refer to the popular edition in twelve volumes, Heinrich Heines Sämmtliche Werke ; Bibliothek Ausgabe. Hamburg : Hoffman & Campe.

THE FAMILY LIFE OF
HEINRICH HEINE

———

THE family life of Heinrich Heine has been falsely depicted in various ways and his relations to his nearest kindred have been often woefully twisted. Yielding to the wishes of his many admirers and in order that the character of the poet might be estimated with more exactness, my mother, now well on in years, who is the only sister of Heinrich Heine, has laid on me this task. She asks that his letters to the family shall be published during her lifetime, letters which she has guarded hitherto as a precious legacy enhanced by all the memories of her beloved brother.

Throughout his entire life apart from his family Heinrich Heine kept up a regular correspondence with his mother and sister, but with his brothers after the emigration to Paris he had

only the most superficial epistolary connection.

Born the thirteenth of December 1799 at Düsseldorf, Heinrich Heine died the seventeenth of
February 1856 in Paris, and for these thirty-six
years past has lain in his tomb in the cemete.y of
Montmartre.

Since the departure of the poet how many
things have changed and what tremendous political revolutions have occurred! The ideal dreams
of the future which he cherished have come true ;
gone is that narrow town-provincialism with its
vexations and absolutism that so often roused
his gibes ; and a newborn Germany has bound together the separate states into a great, powerful
nation.

Heine's satire was never aimed at the ideal, but
always at the crude remnants of individualism and
religious intolerance, especially at the champions
of these survivals who stood out against the im-
pulse of the people toward progress.   The poet's
instinct for freedom and truth inspired him to
depict with irony and the shrillest colors the
discordant shades of the time and all the con-
trasts and contradictions which spring from a

narrow view of the world; he must illumine with his humor the follies of society and relentlessly drive them back into the caves where they were born.

Heine's enemies feel themselves hurt down to the very present time in their small-souled reactionary views by the work he accomplished so long ago. Purposely ignoring his zeal as a reformer, they judge him according to things as they now exist, and cast suspicion on his patriotism. This is a piece of fault-finding all the more unjust, since in his verses and writings the poet often bemoaned his exile and drew a picture of his yearning for Germany:

> Ah, Germany, far-off and dear,
> I well nigh weep at thoughts of thee!
> Meseems that joyous France is drear,
> Her giddy people weary me.*

Samson Heine, father of the poet, was born in Hanover in 1765 and came to Düsseldorf in 1796; there he learned to know intimately a notable family, the Van Gelderns, and on the sixth of June 1798 he married their daughter

---

* See vol. ii. p. 80 of the edition called the Bibliothek-Ausgabe. For Heine's sketch of his father see vol. v. pp. 289-300.—TR.

Betty. From this wedlock sprang three sons, Heinrich, Gustav and Max, and one daughter, Charlotte.

Samson Heine established his hearth in Düsseldorf, and it is quite likely that the house in the Völkerstrasse, which bears the marble memorial plaque, indicates correctly the spot where stood the dwelling in which Heine was born. But not a stone remains of the old house, which was built more than a century before; twice have houses been torn down and rebuilt there. The sister of Heine, when she heard that the tenants of the present house showed to strangers, as the birthplace of Heinrich Heine, two rooms in a rear building in the nature of a stable reached by a narrow ladder for poultry, declared publicly at the time that this part of the house was never used at all by her parents and the poet's cradle could never have stood there.

After he had passed through the classes of the lyceum at Düsseldorf, the young Heinrich, whose intellectual development even as a boy gave rise to the brightest hopes, was destined by his parents, but against his own inclination, to mer-

cantile pursuits. After several attempts which
showed no results the parents became convinced
that he had poor qualifications for this career;
then they yielded to his wishes and allowed him
to study. Having terminated a course in the
"gymnasium" preparatory for college, he entered Bonn University toward the end of the
year 1819. After a short stay in Oldesloe his
family emigrated to Lüneburg, and after this pilgrimage his sister received from him the following letter :

I

BONN, March 22, 1820.

DEAR LITTLE CHARLOTTE:

I rely greatly on all my [home] letters. You
must write me how all things are with you there
[at Lüneburg] and just what happened when you
left [Oldesloe]. The hall of the Musical Society
must have been hung with black crape ; I'm sure
that for a fortnight not an *allegro* was heard
there—only *adagio*. And then the streets—how
dead and alive must they be now! Did you
shed tears when you left ? How did you get on
during the journey? Many a night have I sat

on my wooden chair and mechanically read on
in my big, learned books, and all the while my
thoughts were wandering about over Lüneburg
Heath, and were anxiously looking out to see:
if perchance your driver were not asleep; if your
wagon were really on the right track; if your
wheel had not broken.

Are you worthy that I should so love you?

HARRY HEINE,
stud. juris.

After staying a year in Bonn, Heinrich went
to Göttingen, and the year after sought Berlin,
where in 1821 he caused himself to be matric-
ulated as student in the university. He read law
and finance, but, notwithstanding this somewhat
dry work, he remained true to his poetic instincts
and produced songs and romances in abundance.
His sojourn in Berlin and his intimate relations
with the best literary circles of the capital continued to develop his literary activity. His publications soon roused a general sensation, and at
this period lies the beginning of his fame as a
poet.

His sister Charlotte, who was staying in Ham-

burg at the house of her uncle, engaged herself
to Moritz Embden, a merchant of that town,* and
as a sequel to a joyous festival held by the
family to honor the event, the latter received the
following epistle :

II

BERLIN, February 2, 1823.

DEAR EMBDEN :

Your letter of the twenty-third of last month
has filled me with great joy.   I congratulate you
on the engagement to my sister.   Although the
news agitates me very much, certainly far more
than anyone could have suspected, yet it did not
come upon me as a "singular whim of fate";
rather did it seem to me a fact of which I had
long been aware, and indeed known many
years ago, but one which I had gradually forgot
during the storms of life within me and without.

I hope that you and my sister will be a happy
pair, since Lotta is perfectly capable of feeling
the worth of your character, and since you also
understand how to appreciate the character of my

* Moritz Embden, born 1790, died 1866. left one son and two
daughters.

sister. Moreover, you will certainly not esteem too much, as occurs in our fine, overcultured world, a one-sided predominance in a woman of intellect, or of heart, or of body ; if I judge you aright, you will certainly recognize true culture only in a beautiful balance of all the attributes of the soul and recognize real lovableness in a harmony of soul and body. My little Lotta is music—all proportion and harmony . . . a brother need not forbear to utter such sentiments to the bridegroom.

The political portion of your letter has pleased me much. I am glad that the future husband of my sister is not a revolutionist. Moreover, I find it most natural that a man who is *à son aise* and a happy bridegroom too, should not desire the fall of existing forms, and is anxious about his quiet and that of Europe. Other circumstances govern me, and besides, I feel a little queer whenever I read by chance in the papers that a few people have frozen to death on the streets of London, a few persons have starved to death in the streets of Naples. Still, though I'm a Radical in England and a Carbonaro in Italy, I do not belong to the demagogues in Germany,

for the entirely fortuitous and insufficient reason
that upon the victory of these people a few
thousand Jewish necks—and just the best ones
of all—would be promptly sliced off.

Meantime let our views upon the events of
the day be as sharply separated as they will,
or even quite opposed to each other, I am nevertheless convinced that this will not exercise in
the slightest degree an unfriendly pressure on
our friendship as near relatives, which even at
a distance (for a sullen dislike will always keep
me away from Hamburg) will often brighten,
teach and rest me by genial sympathy, intelli-
gent explanations and loving stimulation; for I
live ever out of sorts and in the midst of error
and battle.

H. HEINE.

III

BERLIN, May 3, 1823.

DEAR EMBDEN:

I have your letter of April 28 all right and
hasten to fulfill your desire to see my tragedies
at the same time that I have the honor to
send you the inclosed copy as a proof of my

regard. May the booklet find a welcome in your
home and may the ethical bases of the matter
not be ignored by you! You shall read in this
book how men perish and races of men, and
yet how this destruction is caused and controlled
by a higher necessity and has been purposely
arranged by Providence for great objects and
aims.* The true poet does not give the history
of his own times, but that of all times, and for
that reason a true poem is also ever a mirror of
the present.

One of these days I'm going to Lüneburg,
but at this moment I am very *malade* and
write these lines suffering the most awful
pains.

I send you hearty greeting.

H. HEINE.

Soon after the marriage of his sister, which
took place June 22, 1823, Heine went to Ritzebüttel for his health in order to take sea baths in
Cuxhaven, because he had contracted nervous
headaches through overwork.

* Heine's " William Ratcliff," a tragedy in one act (1822).

IV

RITZEBÜTTEL, July 28, 1823.

DEAR LOTTA:

Here I am! Can't say more owing to wretched health. I shall take the whole cure here. About the first days of September I shall be through with it. If a letter comes for me, send it to me addressed H. Heine from Berlin, lodging at the Harmony in Ritzebüttel. There are few people here, *triste* and *ennuyant.* And everything frightfully dear. I pay out daily more than six marks, and it's impossible to get along cheaper. Notify mother where I am. Greetings to Moritz and to all who ask after me.

If you can write me something to brighten me, do let me hear!

Your loving brother

H. HEINE.

Sea baths did Heine's health good, and after a short stay in Hamburg at his sister's house he went on to Lüneburg for a visit of a few months to his parents.

V

LÜNEBURG, September 15, 1823.

DEAR BROTHER-IN-LAW AND SISTER:

Yesterday evening I reached here sound and well, and have found my dear parents sound and well also.

I left Hamburg at one o'clock—good weather and a quick passage. Here is the same old grumpy Lüneburg, seat of boredom! Little Ami* was quite beside himself with joy! Mother was not a little frightened, dear Lotta, when she learned of your mishap. I told her that her last letter with good counsel came too late, and that although time is lost her grandmotherly hopes would still be fulfilled. I had to tell a lot about you; that you can readily suppose. The thumbscrews were put to me in proper fashion! I have given a description of your maidservant to mother and she counsels you, dear Lotta, not to get rid of this girl; when you got the third maid you would begin to regret the first. You can scarcely imagine, dear Lotta, how much mother thinks

---

*A lap dog of which Heine was fond. See verses to a Möpschen, vol i. p. 233.—TR.

about you, day and night! She is surprised that you have become violent and believes that it comes from your way of living, from the spiced and fat dishes.

I could not tell them enough as to your appearance. With delight I was able to tell, dear Embden, that you love my sister with all your heart, always taking pains for her, supporting her foibles, bearing in manly fashion her little caprices, willingly dispensing with your own whims and always showing yourself a trusty husband. Verily, my friends, I reckon as nothing your little skirmishes; that is omnipresent; the loftiest moment of wedlock is a battle and even a bloody one. It really means nothing if the wife shows her teeth, so long as the teeth are nice and white; if she sheds tears, so long as they become her; and if she stamps angrily with her feet, so long as they are sweetly small. And what is more blissful than forgiveness? And Moritz is so kind-hearted!

Yes, dear Embden, your heart is, 'tis true, full of corners, but it is sound, and as to the rest of your character I had to admire and love it more and more, although its angularities are uncommon and my character is quite otherwise planned. I hope that in the future we shall come nearer together in all geniality, and that you too may find out and recognize the good which often lies hidden away in me. I have already given you proof that I trust you for possessing in practical life a clear and true view; perhaps some day you will discover that in the ideal life, namely, wherever it is a question of ideas, I have eyes no less sharp and true. At a needful moment you have been very useful to me through your penetration and I am very grateful for it. I must give you good thanks besides for the good soups that I have eaten at your board, the many good glasses of wine I have drunk with you, and the manifold favors which you have so kindly shown me!

Keep me in happy remembrance! Greet heartily all friends. Fare ye well and keep in affection

Your trusty
H. HEINE.

VI

LÜNEBURG, October 12, 1823.

DEAR LOTTA:

Your dear little letter of October 7 duly received last week and sufficiently kissed. Every-

thing you write is so dainty one would say the
most skillful pastry cook had modeled it. Write
to me often ; each time you give me pleasure
thereby. We are all in the best of health.
Mother and father are well. Gustav was in good
condition—only too good. Little Max, the big
pedant, is industrious. But he's orderly nevertheless, and we need fear nothing on his account.
We have a new cook ; the which is most sassy.
I advise you to keep your maidservant. My
head does better every day. How can you believe that I am not purposing to carry out the
prescribed plan of reading law? I love you
beyond all words and yearn for the moment
when I can see you again, since there is no person in the world in whose company I am of better
spirits than in that of my sister. We understand
each other so perfectly; we alone have sense; and
the rest of the world is clean crazed ! Write me
lots, whatever news there is in your place. Be
careful of your health ; this bustling round is not
wholesome for you. Be yielding to your husband ; he is in verity a thoroughly kind fellow.
We two differ in this regard : in his head the
screws are turned too tightly, and in mine they

are screwed too loosely.   I have just received the address for the books; Jan goes to fetch them. It is very borous here, but I am pleased.

Farewell and keep me in affection.

Thy faithful brother,
H. HEINE.

VII

LÜNEBURG, November 7, 1823.

DEAR LOTTA:

You are certainly angry with me!   And still I would not write to you to-day except that I must send you the ticket list which I forgot to place with the books.   Send me some more books soon.   And after all, what were there to to write ?   How we live you know well enough.

I am much honored here.   Especially am I often in society at Superintendent Christiani's; Dr. Christiani has made me famous in all Lüneburg and my verses circulate!   At the same time I am always trying to withdraw from society; my headaches, which will not disappear, and my law studies occupy me too much.

There is no culture here; I believe there is a lightning rod for culture on the town house.

But the people are not so bad. Often do I think
of you, kindly, darling, transparent child! How
often I yearn to kiss your little alabaster paws!
Love me just as hard as you know how!

What you write about Methfessel* pleases me
highly. Remember me heartily to him. I wish
I could hear my songs sung. I must see to it,
anyhow, that I get Klein's music to them. We
are all in good case. Farewell, sweet little doll
of crystal! Knit me a pair of woolen slippers.

> Thy brother, who loves thee,
>
> HARRY HEINE.

VIII

LÜNEBURG, December 8, 1823.

DEAR LITTLE SOUL :

I have not written you for a long time, because
I have been ever waiting for an answer to my
last letter. I ought not to have minded that, and
written all the same ; still I have a good excuse.
Moreover I am in too vile a mood to say anything gay, and you know that when I have my
black hour on I never permit myself to be seen

---

* For a short notice of Albert Methfessel, composer, written
1823, see vol. xii. p. 119.—TR,

by you. You must always see me in the rosiest light and must love me well. Ah, how delighted I am with the news that you are soon to be here ! I hear you already : *yow, yow !* In thought I kiss the sweet tones of your voice.

I shall be glad also to see Moritz. I have to like him when I hear that he loves you so much —as father tells and cannot finish telling. How splendid it is, now that you two have learned to bear with each other's weak sides ! Mutual for-bearance, allowances and understanding lay the foundations of a good marriage. Moritz will know well enough how to treat such a dear, fragile, pretty and lively toy as you are.

I hope you are in good health, dear Lotta. Be quite sure that always I think of you. Don't I know well enough that the good Lord intends that all men shall kiss your hands ? That I be-lieve ; that is my religion.

H. HEINE.

IX

LÜNEBURG, December 26, 1823.

DEAR LOTTA :

'Tis a wrong that cries to heaven that I don't get a line under my eyes from you. How are

you living—how are you getting on? O how
I suffered to have to leave without having,
sweetest creature, seen you again—spoken to
you—kissed you!

All the morning I've been racking my brains
whether it would be one or two fingers that I'd
be glad to sacrifice in order to be able to live a
few years in your neighborhood. I would come
to Hamburg to say good-by to you if I did not
have to run the moral gauntlet there past too
big a crowd of acquaintances.

Write me now and then after I reach Göttingen. Your letters have exactly the stamp of
your neat, pretty soul, and are veritable bon-
bons for my heart! Thoughts of you, dear
sister, will often hold me erect when the great
herd of mankind crushes me with their stupid
hatred and loathsome love.

My greetings for the new year! Congratulations to Moritz also; I will write him from Göttingen. Here I have nothing to report to him
and he is too good a fellow for a commonplace
letter with obligatory watering. Do, pray, congratulate them in my name when you are at
Uncle Salomon Heine's. Remember also me to

Henry Heine, together with the entire Henriade. And if it is not too much trouble, give my regards to all the Embdens.

But before all things fare you well and hold me fast in affection.

H. HEINE.

X

LÜNEBURG, January 9, 1824.

DEAR SMALL PERSON:

To-day I am not off, but to-morrow I journey, if in the meantime my shirts are dry and if the letter arrives which I expect from Berlin. You know from the Hamburg experiences that I readily stick fast wherever I may be. But to-day a week the gates and human faces of Lüneburg must be behind me. Separation from the parents will come hard. We declaim your little piece with trumpet accompaniment: *Calypso ne pouvait se consoler du départ d'Ulysse.* Do you ever think, small Frenchwoman, of that Télémaque period?

How delighted were I to kiss once more your charming cat's paws before I leave this part of the world! Departure from little Ami will also be hard. Truly this small beast has made many an hour bright. Every evening when I read, the trig little creature sits on my shoulder and always begins to bark when we reach a fine passage in the book. Little Ami has more wisdom and feeling than all the German philosophers and poets.

I greatly rejoiced at your letter of the thirty-first of December. Heartily did I laugh at your literary dilemma. Write me often. That I am at work on a tragedy, as people have informed you, is not quite correct.

The fact is, I have not written a line of it, and the piece so far exists only in my head, where many another piece and a lot more good volumes are lying ready. Till now I have been too ill to write anything and the few hours of health I have are devoted to my studies. In truth it is still seed time with me ; but I hope for a good harvest. I try to assimilate the most varied knowledge, and shall for that reason evince my-self all the more cultivated and many-sided an author. The poet is only a small part of me ; I think you have known me long enough to under-stand that. Your counsel to let many deaths

occur in my tragedy has my attention. Good
Lord, I wish I could let all my enemies come to
a bad end in it.*

Greet Moritz from me many thousand times.
Reiterate the assurance of my friendship. Whoever loves my wee, small Lotta, him also do I
love. Besides, I am really a great admirer of
Archenholtz.†

I hope, dear Lotta, you will see that many nice
letters reach me in Göttingen ; each one of them
brightens up my soul. Everything that you write
is so nice and clear; like a burnished mirror
every line shows me your excellent natural
temperament.

Farewell, and hold me in affection.

H. HEINE.

XI

GÖTTINGEN, January 31, 1824.

DEAR, SWEET SISTER :

I hope that these lines will find you in perfect
health. So far as I am concerned I am getting

*For Heine's humorous claim to modesty in wishes, see vol. xii.
p. 193.—TR.

† Perhaps an allusion to Jos. Wilh. Archenholtz, author of
works on England, Italy, the Seven Years' War, etc., who died
near Hamburg in 1812.—TR.

on better than before. I think Lüneburg must
have a bad air : hardly a single hour of health
did I enjoy there. The people, it is true, did
everything to make the nest agreeable, especially at the last. I finished the journey with no
very remarkable events. Lüneburg Heath is
one-third of eternity and bored me quite
enough and through weariness of spirit I made
rhymes—yes, rhymes to you, which perhaps some
day I may let you see. They are only a couple of
stanzas. But I love you and think ever of you.

I passed three days in Hanover and got acquainted there with a beautiful lady and was
most agreeable—no other than I ! In my journey hither from Hanover I had bad weather ; it
snowed as if all the heavenly armies were shaking
their feather beds down on me, and what is more,
I sat in a half-open side coach near the master-
at-arms, whose crimson-red mantle gradually
turned to ermine. And I thought of you and I
let it snow in the name of God, and when *trara,
trara*, the postilion on the post wagon rattled
past, my heart was much moved and I thought :
that boy certainly has letters which will reach
Hamburg in three days, and I envied the letters.

I came to Göttingen while I slept. What does that omen mean?

The next morning as I leaned out of the window of the tavern I saw my old bootblack pass and called him up. In comes the whimsical fellow without uttering a word, and brushes my clothes and boots without speaking a word, and does not show the slightest surprise at my being away from Göttingen for three years; my old orders that he must never speak in my presence and never ask a question have never been forgotten.

I have few acquaintances here and the professors are not particularly fond of me, because when I was rusticated here I sent cards of farewell in a mocking tone to the members of the Academical Senate.

I'm up to the neck in juristic studies and things roll along. I found it a bit of luck that, although I have come in the middle of a term, I can hear a good deal on subjects for which I have not come too late.

Farewell, beauteous lady, and keep me in happy memory and write me oft. My address is H. Heine, *cand. juris*, on the Rothenstrasse at

Widow Brandissen's in Göttingen. Greet all acquaintances for me and write how everything looks and whether the tarts have come out good this year. If you cook or bake anything, put it aside for me until I get round to see you. But you yourself are more dear to me than all the tarts on this globe, not excepting even lemon tarts!

I would like to write you more, but it is too dusky in my brains and anyhow I could not express at all how heartily devoted to you is

Your brother,

H. HEINE.

XII

GÖTTINGEN, March 30, 1824.

DEAR LOTTA:

I have received your and Moritz's letter all right and seen with pleasure that you are both well and in a happy frame of mind. Tell Moritz I am very glad to hear that he remembers me in kindness and that I shall write to him before long. Nor shall I give you, dear Lotta, a real and actual reply to-day; the purpose of this letter is merely to inform you that I propose to

make a flying trip to Berlin this week in order
to pass there a part of the present vacation; that
presently I am sure to be able to write something
more interesting and that if you wish to have
anything done for you in Berlin, you must write
it out for me at length, directing H. Heine from
Düsseldorf, care of M. Friedländer & Co., on the
new Friedrichstrasse, No. 47 in Berlin.

The reason for this trip is composed of a
thousand little by-reasons; amusement is certainly
the least of them all.   Meantime the movement
and the change in such a trip is very good for my
head.   I hope, dear Lotta, that you too are in
good health and love me still.   My Muse is fur-
ished with a muzzle so as not to bother me with
her melodies while threshing the straw of jurispru-
dence.   Yet not so long ago I sent off a cyclus
of little poems for *Der Gesellschafter** and gave
orders that they should send two copies to you
in Hamburg and I want you to give one copy to
Uncle Henry.   Don't forget this.   And be so
good as to say to Uncle Henry that his letter
reached me and the credit was paid me all right.
As you may imagine, you must do this at once

* A widely read periodical published by Professor Gubitz.

and may add that I am on a journey and will for that reason write later on. Don't forget this either, by the soul of you! because Uncle Henry has shown me much kindness and favor and I owe him much gratitude.

Yesterday I had a letter from Lüneburg and heard that Theresa Heine * had been sick of the smallpox and was convalescent. Tell me if she suffered much. It would pain me greatly. Send my best regards to that dear maid as well as to the rest of the clan.

As to my health I am still unable to boast a great deal, but it will do. I am in a tide of correspondence with Lüneburg and write often. You know it gives father and mother pleasure and a double pleasure to dear father, because he goes for the letters himself. Of you, dear, sweet wifelet, I think constantly; would I could see you in your present rounded shape! Already there stirs in me the suspicion of avuncular feelings, and I am on tenterhooks whether I shall get a nephew or a niece. O what a happy man will Moritz be when he hears the first cry of the child! How it will smell of cookies in mamma's

* Youngest daughter of Salomon Heine for whom the poet has been accused of *Cousinenschwärmerei*. See note p. 137.—TR.

house! Everybody will be delighted and bustle about, and in the first moment Aunt Jette * will not know whether she has become an aunt or really a great-aunt.

But in order that all these things come to pass take care of yourself, dear child, and keep in affection

Your brother,

H. HEINE.

XIII

GÖTTINGEN, May 8, 1824.

BELOVED SISTER:

All I'll do to-day is to notify you that I have reached Göttingen again sound and well and that I expect to get from you a letter full of particulars as to how you are. Everything else is side-issue—I only want to know how you feel. When do you expect to be delivered? Now do you perceive what a good thing it is to have learned to add and subtract? Spare yourself in all things, do not run much, don't eat trash, or else your child will be a nibbler of sweets, and also do not read any verses, or else the child you bear will be a poet—which may well be called a

* The wife of Henry Heine was the sister of Moritz Embden.

great piece of bad luck. I forgot your present
condition; otherwise I should never have sent
you the thirty-three songs.

My trip up to Berlin was made in bad weather;
it was cold and snowed horribly. The journey
back was much better, in fine weather and forty-
eight hours—so swiftly flies the lightning post! *

It was most surprising to see the Harz Moun-
tains, which I had left covered with snow, already
clad in the most genial of spring verdure. It was
in the Harz indeed that I saw a lady who looked
very like you in features and in general appearance.

It was this way. I drove from Stollberg to
Harzgerode over a tall, snow-clad hill, where the
coach threatened every moment to upset—a perilous, dreary ride. Now about midnight when
we reached the posthouse at Harzgerode we
found the waiting room half full of passengers
who had come, some of them by other post
coaches, others by special coach, and there they
were, drinking coffee, putting their furs off and
on, quarreling in loud voices with the postmaster,

---

* At that time the first lightning post coaches were introduced
into Germany through the efforts of the Prussian postmaster-
general von Nagler.

cursing the weather and making faces like the day after a debauch.

Near the stove, which was not particularly warm, sat a marvelous-lovely woman who seemed exceeding distinguished, but, alas, most disgusted—and she looked precisely as you do when you are in a cantankerous mood! Why, she looked like cantankerousness itself when she learned from our postilion that the road to Stollberg was so vile; and a dainty gentleman in a magnificent fur coat, who wound wheedling about her in an anxious deprecatory way, watching for her slightest nod, had to support the entire flood of her grumpiness. Half crying, half scolding, she said to him : "Why did you not kill me outright before it came to this? Didn't you know that I am sick?" and so forth.

I tried as well as I could to comfort the angry lady and warbled,

O, what pleasure travel brings !

from "Jean de Paris." When she heard that, the sweetest little melancholy smile crossed her pretty, vexed countenance; she rowed with less violence that wretched, natty gentleman in the fur

coat, and when presently the latter offered her
his arm and led her gracefully to the coach, she
turned again and again to me with farewell bows;
she sighed and warbled,

O, what pleasure travel brings !

To-day these words have been ringing in my
ears the entire morning and so I have told you
the adventure.   But should I talk about Berlin I
would not be so quickly done.   Only this much
will I say, that I am still held in sufficient love
and respect by the people there.   They wondered
not a little moreover that through love of work
I should select for my abode wearisome Göttingen
instead of fascinating Berlin.   And people wondered still more that I was able to leave at the
proper time in order not to be late for lectures
here in Göttingen.   In Berlin I passed many a
charming hour and absorbed much spiritual stir
and refreshment, and assuredly this journey was
in every respect useful to me.

Thanks, dearest Lotta, for your kindness in
carrying out my commission with Uncle Henry;
you would make me grateful again if once more
you would give my greeting to kind Uncle

Henry. For in the restless agitation in which I have been—inwardly and outwardly—up till the present moment I was not able to reach the point of writing to our kind uncle; so it is important for me that he should learn I did not stay too long in Berlin and that the trip was healthful to body and soul.

Just now I feel better than I have known myself for a year and a day. If it is possible, I shall write to-day to Lüneburg. How is Uncle Salomon Heine? I was not a little scared when I heard not long ago that everybody at Uncle Heine's was so ill. Thank God they are in good health again! I am glad that I did not know it before. I beg you to write me the particulars, how they are now. My address is H. Heine, *stud. juris* from Düsseldorf in Göttingen.

My regards to Moritz; part of this letter is meant for him; I think of him often and with pleasure. Write to me soon and keep me in affection. You cannot possibly believe how heartily I love you!

Thy brother,
H. HEINE.

XIV

GÖTTINGEN, August 9, 1824.

DEAR FATHER MORITZ:

I cannot utter to you the delight I felt in mother's lines and your postscript! I congratulate you on the coming of the sweet little daughterlet and trust that she will become a copy of her sweet little mother. Day and night was I forced to think of our dear Lotta; my thoughts were ever at the Neuenwall in one of the dainty rooms. For some time, dear Moritz, I have observed that you are discovering day by day more exactly the secret, how one can live happy with our dear Lotta and make her a happy woman. I knew well enough that so clever and honest a man as you are would end by getting to the bottom of the secret, just as I knew that so dear a child as our Lotta would always show herself lovable and childishly docile, if a person only treated her properly; in fact, like an adored child.

Now a new bond has knit you together in union and happiness; the sweet creature to whom you two have given life will be a fresh source of new gladness and love. And I too, Moritz, am bound closer to you through a fresh family chain: your daughter is my niece. May Heaven keep in good health both the beings whom we love so much, mother and daughter!

So far as I am concerned, my health gets on better all the while; very slowly to be sure. I am exclusively occupied with my law studies and think of taking a degree in January. I am quite certain that in a few years my headaches will vanish and that then I shall be able better than now to work hard and to live.

To my sweetest Lotta I send the heartiest greetings. I cannot tell her enough how sweet and delightsome her last letter was. I kissed every line, and then read again and kissed once more. I beg you to congratulate Lotta in my name and kiss her hand.

If possible I shall write to-day to our dear mother. How she must rejoice! I have guests here just now, namely Brother Max, who is with me on a visit. We can never reach the end of our talks about you two. I send my congratulations to your mother and brothers.

I beg you not to give the child a "precious"

name; give her a simple, genuine German one. Fare ye well and hold me in affection.

I am,

Your brother,

H. HEINE.

XV

GÖTTINGEN, May 11, 1825.

DEAR BROTHER-IN-LAW :

You have real occasion to be very angry with me and I really do not know how I can excuse my long silence. The only thing I shall put forward is that I have failed to write neither from neglect nor indifference. I am always thinking of my sister and consequently of all things connected with her and consequently of my brother-in-law. But I love you too well to embitter an hour of your time with long descriptions of the miserable situation of a sickly, grumpy man, plagued by God and the world. Certainly you are too dear to me to write you empty words or perchance lies! So then, let a kind brother-in-law and his small wife forgive my long silence.

But now I am able to write you ; my health im-

proves—it was very wretched—and at the same
time the clouds raise a little from my outer
life.

All the past winter I dug away at jurispru-
dence without let up, and so last week was in
condition to take the examination of doctor of
laws, which I passed in fine shape. This is the
capital point with regard to degree taking ; all the
rest—for example, disputation—is empty form
and scarcely worthy of mention. So practically
I am a doctor, and it has no longer an ironical
effect when you call me that in your letters.
But I shall not dispute for six weeks to come, because in the first place there's no hurry, as I shall
remain here.till Michaelmas, and in the second
I want to finish writing my disputation. This is
the best news I can impart—everything else is
still in the dark. You can easily explain to
yourself moreover why I spare you the facts
concerning my external affairs which, as with
everybody, depend on economical conditions.
People may complain as they will of my folly and
chaotic state, but I know that I think and act as
befits my inner self-respect. Dear Moritz, I have
my well established jury for whatever I do—but

this jury is not yet assembled to act as the
judge over me. Merchants are scarcely apt to
be among them.

I hope that this letter finds you sound and
gay. As I hear that Lotta is about to journey
to Lüneburg, I shall write to the dear little wife
there. Kiss for small Marilet! How curious I
am to see her!

Whether I shall establish myself in Hamburg?
That is known to the gods who created hunger.
I shall not settle down there without being
provided with bread for a couple of years. Meantime on my side everything will be done; baptized * and a DOCTOR JURIS, and 'tis hoped in
good health, I shall presently arrive in Hamburg.
I would not write you all this if you had not often
asked to know.

Fare ye well; keep me in love, and be assured
that from my heart I am

Your devoted brother-in-law,

H. HEINE.

* At that period no Jew could receive a degree at law, or practice. It was customary for Jews like Heine, on whom their special religion lay very slack, to pronounce the formulas of Christian
baptism like that of taking a degree, holding that the shame lay
with those who baptized.—TR.

XVI

GÖTTINGEN, July 31, 1825.

DEAR LOTTA:

I have heard from father that you left the flowery meads of Lüneburg long ago and find yourself once more in Hamburg the blessed. So far as I am concerned, as you see, I am still in that learned cowstable Göttingen, where I disputed in public on the twentieth of the present month for the degree of doctor of laws. They must have sent you this piece of news from Lüneburg. I thought you were there, otherwise I should have written to you before.

I have asked Max to send my theses* from Berlin to Moritz ; I should have written him by this had I considered it worth while to make much talk about the winning of a doctor's degree.

Greet Moritz heartily for me, and if you are

---

*The Latin disquisition by H. Heine contained contentions on the following subjects: 1. The husband is master of the dowry. 2. The creditor must produce a receipt. 3. All judicial acts are to be performed in public. 4. No binding duty springs from an oath. 5. Among the Romans *confarreatio* was the most ancient form of legal wedlock.

certain he is no blab, say to him that I am now not only a *Doctor Juris*, but also ———— ————.*
Yesterday it rained just as it did six weeks ago. When the longest day occurred a little while ago I thought of the Zollenspiker † at Hamburg, and solemnized the occasion with perspiration and thoughts of you two.

For the last two years you have known our Moritz quite intimately enough to tell whether he can keep his mouth shut and so forth. Day before yesterday I ate fine strawberries; they lay most sweetly on the sugar and I duly covered them well up.

I don't know how long I shall remain here, and whether I shall not within the next few days leave town and make another trip afoot. In any case I shall be in Lüneburg the middle of September in order to see the parents, and thence my way leads to —— I really do not yet know if it will be possible for me to stick fast in Hamburg. To be sure, I do not feel so badly off in health any more; thank God, my constitution is stronger

* Play upon Heine's baptism into the Lutheran Church, June 28, 1825.
† Where the wedding of his sister was celebrated.

than it was; but I am still enough of a sick man to think more about the present than the future. In no circumstances shall I come to Hamburg if means of subsistence are not assured me beforehand.

If this is not the case, then provisionally I choose Berlin, where there are more chances of gain open to me at once. If only I could have have the consciousness, dear Lotta, that you are contented with me, and perceive that on my part I have done everything by which I believed it possible to arrange to live in your beloved neighborhood.

Be assured that no pleasure, no champagne, no theater, no tickling of vanity and no glance from lovely woman were so much to my heart as a cozy, gossipy stay with you, dear, lovable child! You know well enough how I am—how livable, how docile and contented with little! You and two other stately ladies know that very well and understand how to value it.

I beg you to walk a great deal lest you get too fat! I pray you—do not become a Hamburg woman! Greet and kiss for me your little girl. And write me soon. Just send the letters to Lüneburg; I will write to father as soon as I leave, to say whither he shall send them.

Remember me to our Gustav, at last in Hamburg for good and all. I send inclosed the theses on which I disputed, which you may impart to Gustav or to any other learned person you please.

Farewell, and keep me in affection.

Your brother,

H. HEINE.

The frontispiece is one little known and was drawn by a friend of Heine's youth, during his first stay in Göttingen. It was held in high honor by his sister owing to the strong resemblance; the youthful bust carved by Professor Herter in 1890 at Berlin is very like it.

At this period my mother depicted her brother as follows: " His appearance was more youthful than his age would lead one to expect; he was without beard until his incurable illness began; the delicate, almost maiden-like features of his pale, oval face were set in a background of light brown hair. His mouth would twist itself in a satirical smile when he repeated a joke or witticism, and the grayish blue eyes, at other times somewhat dull, began to sparkle. Of medium stature and always elegantly clad, his whole being expressed an aristocratic something. He was always very active and industrious and went regularly to lectures. The habits of students never had his sympathy; he did not smoke, drank no beer, very little wine, and although member of a *Burschenschaft*, avoided all nocturnal banquets."

After taking his doctor's degree Heine was very undecided whether he should choose Hamburg or Berlin for a continued residence. He had many friends in Berlin, and in particular there were two social circles which exercised a great attraction on him. The house of the poetess Elisa von Hohenhausen was the gathering place of all the *beaux esprits;* and this woman of genius, an enthusiastic admirer of Lord Byron, whose poems she had in part translated, was the first to recognize Heine's high poetic gift; she called him the German Byron and proclaimed that in him her ideals had been born again.*

* For translations of " Manfred " and short poems by Byron, see vol. i. pp. 214–227.—Tr.

The second circle, which assisted his poetic
evolution more, was that ruled by Varnhagen
von Ense, whose brilliant wife Rahel, the latter's
brother Robert and his beautiful wife, formed
Heine's most intimate surroundings. In this
house there was an altar raised to Goethe, and a
lively propaganda was carried on there to obtain
a true understanding and valuation of his works.
Owing to their exaggerated worship everything
was brought into comparison with him ; notwithstanding the very different direction the works
of the two poets took, a certain relationship with
the poetic method of Goethe was extracted from
Heine's poems.

In his diary Max Heine * describes the Berlin
friends of that period ; he tells how he came
bearing a letter of introduction to Moses Moser,
to that trusty and noble friend of Heinrich
Heine, that very friend, in fact, to whom were
addressed the poet's letters, to-day full of
laughter, to-morrow of wailings.

Moser was partner in the wealthy banking
house of M. Friedländer & Co., and was self-
taught and a philanthropist in the noblest sense

---

* The brother who entered the Russian Service as a surgeon.
He wrote a number of books of travel and biography.—Tr.

of the word. He used every spare hour for solid
studies and his many-sidedness was a subject for
remark. Apart from his thorough knowledge of
almost all tongues, he read Plato, Homer, Tacitus,
Shakspere, Cervantes, Dante in the original; he
carried on studies in Sanskrit and was entirely at
home in astronomy, philosophy and belles lettres.

"With the letters of introduction from Heinrich in one hand" wrote Max Heine "and Mr.
Moser on the other, I entered that large
circle of families whose members were among
the most gifted and illustrious of mankind.
First it was Varnhagen von Ense, famous
from his critical and biographical writings—an
acknowledged model as German stylist. The
soul of his house was the celebrated Rahel,
Varnhagen's gifted wife ; she it was who dubbed
the young, high-spirited poet with the Aristo-
phanic nickname of 'naughty favorite of the
Graces.' In this house the intellectual moun-
tain tops of Berlin were to be met, and all the
arts and sciences were represented. Wilhelm
and Alexander von Humboldt, the great philosopher Hegel, the immortal sculptor Rauch,
Schleiermacher, Hitzig, Chamisso and the

brother of Rahel, Ludwig Robert, famed as a poet, together with his ideally beautiful wife Friederike, were like many others constant guests.

"Quite another circle, which formed a world to itself, was offered me by the Veit household which stood in interesting connection with the history of intellectual and commercial Berlin. Head of a well-known business house, he gathered about him every week a circle of men who on such evenings set before them the task of furnishing an entertainment richly spiced with wit. The leaders of this circle were almost all of them personal and true friends of Heinrich Heine. Moser and the celebrated jurist Professor Gans were guests never absent. Dr. Rosenhain too, the botanist, the clever writer Daniel Lessmann, and Joseph Lehmann, publisher and editor of the *Magazine for Foreign Literature*, whose chief contributor Lessmann was.

"Lehmann, the oldest friend of Heinrich Heine, had been an admirer of the poet from the moment of his first appearance; it was he who, under the name in anagram of Anselmi, furnished the first critical notices of Heine's poems. His able parodies of the latter have been indeed

often taken for poems by Heine. In his widely
read periodical Lehmann followed trustingly on
through the entire literary life of Heine ; he often
illustrated Heine's beautiful passages and always
understood how to unite in the most kindly manner a hearty friend and a stern, incorruptible critic.

" I must mention a few more families in which
I and my brother Heinrich met with the kindliest
reception and where every week an intellectual
society came together.

" Dr. Leopold Zunz, for instance, the great
Orientalist and editor of the much read and
influential *Haude und Spenerschen Zeitung.* He
was himself a member of the friendly circle about
Veit, where the so-called ' Zunz wit' sped in
jovial fashion from mouth to mouth.

" Moser took me also to the Mendelssohn
house and I listened with ecstasy to the playing
of young Felix and did not imagine at the time
that later such ' songs without words ' would pro-
ceed from this boy's head and that Heine's
words would be published with such music !

" I must also recall Albert von Chamisso, a man
extraordinarily beloved, who, though by birth a
Frenchman, stands among the leaders of German

lyricists. At his house I came to know the criminal counselor Hitzig, Chamisso's notable biographer. Hitzig was always a warm friend of Heinrich Heine, with whose youth as a poet he has shown the most lively sympathy. Owing to his good offices the tragedies of Heine appeared in the press of Ferdinand Dümmler. The same may be said of Professor Gubitz, who at that time edited the paper *Gesellschafter für Geist und Herz.* I often took small poems by Heine to him; indeed, he had introduced the poet to the German public by means of the *Gesellschafter* and brought him the booksellers Maurer as publishers of his first collection of poems."

In spite of all the allurements which a residence in Berlin had for Heine, love for his relatives drew him toward Hamburg; after a longer stay in Norderney he made a visit to his parents in Lüneburg ˙in order to talk over his affairs with them.

XVII

LÜNEBURG, October, 1826.

MY DEAR LOTTA

may consider herseıı heartily greeted and assured of my brotherly love! Verily I have remembered you oftener than you would believe and far more tenderly (particularly in these later days) than I myself thought possible. At Norderney I read in a Hamburg journal of your confinement, and of a verity before I read that I had less quiet nerves. I am delighted that you have a boy! May God keep the dear child in his special protection, so that the human thing in him shall not be crippled too early!

Dear Lotta, wherever I may happen to be, my heart is poured out daily in the most loving and pious wishes for you and your children. May things ever go smoothly with you and them! Only be good and you will be happy, and then your children will be good and happy too. I pray you, do not forget me, for I love you much.

Your brother,

H. HEINE.

At the beginning of November Heine reached Hamburg in order to settle down there as a lawyer; but in a very little time he gave up this plan and devoted himself entirely to the profession of an author.

The first part of the "Reisebilder" brought out with Campe, had made its appearance, and the literary result, glorious beyond all measure, may have contributed not a little to the giving up of the dry legal career hardly begun.

The effect made by this book was truly sensational. The humorous, intellectual and original method of his prose style, just like the novel metrical structure of his verse, induced a tremendous revolution in German literature ; imitated by many, it ruled their style for a long period.

Heinrich Heine lived very retired in Hamburg ; his parents had emigrated thither from Lüneburg and he had relations with few families beside theirs, the house of his sister and those of his two uncles. He gave his whole time to finishing the second part of the "Reisebilder." This book also had the same remarkable success as the first.

In the spring of 1827, soon after the appearance of the last mentioned book, Heine went to England * and stayed there three months. He wrote, "that London overtopped his expectations with respect to its enormous size, but that he came near giving himself up for lost there. Nothing

* For " Englische Fragmente," see vol. vi. pp. 221–302.—TR,

but fog, coal smoke, porter and Canning—and so fearfully wet and uncomfortable! The eternal roast beef and leg of mutton, the vegetables as God made them—and Heaven guard everybody from their sauces! Send a philosopher to London; by your life, no poet!" On his return trip Heine passed through Holland to Norderney and returned to Hamburg at the end of September.

First appeared the "Buch der Lieder," which the entire public received with enthusiastic plaudits and which to-day is still considered the most brilliant product of Heine's muse. But many critics of that period who believed that the old metrical method of German poesy was insulted, were only able to see in these melodious rhymes in the nature of folk songs an artificial metre without style.

The objections which were raised against Heine that he neglected the classic forms was very unjust, and are often repeated when anything new and unaccustomed is created. Heine did not write sketchily and without care, but laid uncommon stress upon stylistic finish of expression. In almost all the sketches among his manuscripts which I have read through, there is hardly a page on which changes and improvements have not been made.

Heine at the time of his settlement in Hamburg had always yielded to the vague hope that he would get a position there as a syndic, or else in Prussia as a professor. But in these desires he found himself disappointed. He resolved to consider a permanent engagement as journalist opened up by Baron Cotta and at the end of the year betook himself to Munich. Cotta wished to make a positive engagement with Heine as editor and co-worker on the *Politische Annalen.* Heine however, who wrote several essays for the *Annalen,* was willing to make a permanent engagement for six months only, because great prospects were shown him concerning a chair as professor in the Munich University.

The Minister at that time, Eduard von Schenk, who took a lively interest in the poet and gave him his friendship, felt quite certain that Heine could procure the desired professorship by his aid. Warmly recommended by him to the king, who found great pleasure in reading Heine's works, the decision lay with Ludwig I. The decree of nomination was already written and he would have received the place through the favor of the art-loving monarch, had not Jesuitical whispers undermined the plan. Slanders and too liberal remarks of the poet caught up by eavesdroppers were brought to the king; these put the monarch in bad humor and spoiled the signing of the decree. Out of temper, Heine left that Beery Athens, as he called Munich, and carried out his long cherished resolve of visiting Italy.* He was accompanied as far as the Tyrol by his brother Max, who was a student in Munich.

After he had examined the monuments and galleries in Verona, Milan and Genoa, he reached the baths of Lucca at the end of September, coming by way of Leghorn. The wild and romantic situation of Lucca among the Apennines delighted him and determined him to stay four weeks for the hot baths. Deploring his defective knowledge of Italian, he wrote:

"I don't understand the people and cannot talk with them. I see Italy, but do not hear her. Still I am often not without all enter-

* For the Italian journey, see Reisebilder II., in vol. vi. pp. 1–211. For savage verses on Ludwig I. and his son Otto, temporarily King of Greece, see vol. ii. pp. 114–118, etc.—Tʀ.

tainment. The very stones speak here and I understand their silent tongue. Any broken column belonging to the days of Rome, any moldering tower of the Lombards, any weather-worn clustered Gothic pier knows very well what I mean. Many a time the old palaces want to whisper something to me in secret; but I cannot hear their answer by day owing to the hollow noises of life; then I come back in the night and the moon proves a good interpreter who understands a lapidary style; she knows how to translate into the dialect of my heart. Ay, at night I can understand Italy perfectly; then the new young people with their new opera language sleep and the ancients ascend from their cool couches and speak to me in the most polished Latin."

In Florence, the art-loving city of the Medicis, Heine stayed almost six weeks intoxicated by the art treasures and picture galleries; postponing his visit to Rome, he journeyed back by way of Venice. There he had the sorrowful news of the sudden death of his father, and hastened his return in order to comfort mother and sister for the loss of his warmly beloved father.

He remained in Hamburg with his people till
the next spring and then returned to Berlin, in
order to repeat with the help of his influential
family his efforts to obtain a state appointment.
He dwelt three months at Potsdam in rural
quiet, busily at work on the continuation of the
third volume of the "Reisebilder," and after a
short visit to Helgoland took up his residence
again in Hamburg.

Early in 1830 occurred the publication of the
book; it roused a great sensation. But owing
to its too liberal discussion of the political questions of the day and of affairs of religion, it was
at once proscribed throughout the whole of Germany. Max Heine wrote in this connection in
his diary:

"Among the friends my brother made at the
University of Göttingen was Carl von Raumer,
nephew of the famous historian, writer of the
story of the Hohenstaufens. I was very intimate
with him. He was a highly gifted, poetic and
gushing young fellow, who at that very time was
reading with me enthusiastically the first part of
the 'Reisebilder,' which had just appeared.
Later he became Minister of Public Instruction

in Prussia and in the aberration of his pietism carried it so far as to forbid the sale of Heinrich Heine's work in Prussia; ay, he caused such copies as were seized to be ground up."

Scared, many of his early friends in Berlin drew anxiously into the background, and Heine tried to forget his vexation at many malignant anonymous criticisms in various newspapers among the cool waves of the North Sea off Helgoland. His pain at these attacks could not have been very lasting however, for his sister Charlotte, who was at Ems undergoing treatment because of bad health, received the following letters:

XVIII

HELGOLAND, July 28, 1830.

DEAR LOTTA:

Although a friendly correspondence is a bitter pill to me, and though I have nothing whatever to write except that I love you, still I cannot avoid sending you a couple of lines to the baths. Really I have nothing else to say to you except that I love you and in truth very

greatly! Very often do I think of you—daily
for twenty-five hours, in fact—and my highest
hope is that the trip will restore your health.
Honestly I am oppressed by the fear that your
temperament will lead you to forget your condition and the purpose of the journey, as well as
to cause you to yield to such emotions as may
harm your health yet more. I hope you have
sense enough to remember yourself and your children under circumstances that may occur. Be
sure to avoid evening social gatherings; do not
give way to your temper; be patient and as jolly
as possible. Only in such a frame of mind will the
baths do you good. You see I give you good
rules—but honestly! I myself, though I'm in
similar circumstances, unfortunately do not follow one of them.

I cannot by any means protect myself from the
gloomy state of mind which weighs on me here;
I am in a lively social movement, a thing that
never did me good; chatter far too much; think
too much; eat too much. I have a great deal of
humming and knocking in my ears and my
headaches are at their highest point of bloom.
I have been here three weeks and perhaps shall

stay three weeks longer. There are few Hamburg people here, but among them the Schroe-
ders; we dine together, gallop about the North
Sea all day long, and I like them well enough—
but you I love a thousand times more—ay, a
million times more! I embrace you and hope
to see you again soon. I want to pass the
autumn in your vicinage, since my work seldom
permits me to come to town.* What particularly is going on there *en famille* I do not know
since mother does not write.

Farewell; I kiss you by letter and next
month I shall kiss you by mouth. You need
not write any answer. Next week I shall write
to Immermann and will shove a note for
you into his letter. So on your arrival in
Düsseldorf you can send to Judge Immermann to ask if he has not received a letter for
you. Farewell, sweet woman, and keep me in
affection.

Your faithful brother,

H. HEINE.

* Charlotte von Embden lived at the time in Wandsbeck in the
neighborhood of Hamburg.

XIX

HELGOLAND, August, 1830.

DEAR, SWEET SISTER:

I hope that this letter may still catch you and moreover in much better health. As to mine, it is only so-so. For my trouble bathing in the North Sea is always the most healing thing. Although I have had enough entertainment on Helgoland so far, I think constantly of you nevertheless. Miss Schroeder has departed, but another songstress, the Siebert girl, has arrived and I have a lot of singsong about my ears. With the Schroeder girl I daily quårreled 3 times and made up 1½ times. I shall stay here ten days more and then return to Wandsbeck (or St. Georg) to take up work again. I have no news from Hamburg. If the letter catches you in Düsseldorf still, as I hope, greet uncle and aunt for me most heartily. Be careful of your health ; don't let yourself be vexed and keep me in affection. I trust to seeing you in a fortnight. *Calypso ne pouvait se consoler du départ d'Ulysse !*

It must have been lively in Ems and you, so

to speak, went to meet the French Revolution
halfway. I kiss you.

Your faithful brother,

H. HEINE.

The French Revolution of July, 1830, which
Heine mentioned waggishly in the last letter, was
destined to exert a fateful action on his life ; it
was welcomed by the young poet with plaudits
and exuberant enthusiasm. The fall of Bour-
bon absolutism and the victory of the people's
party wrought upon his spirit in a powerful,
passionate way. Heine expressed this impression in the liveliest fashion in the appendix to
the "Reisebilder," which appeared in 1831 ; also
in the preface to Kahldorf's pamphlet on the
nobility in letters to Count M. von Moltke,
which was written at the same time.* Weary of
the outrages which the poet had to support in
his own land, especially the proscription in
Germany of his writings, his prior plan of carrying out the emigration to France ripened.
At the end of April, with a farewell greeting to
Germany—the poems of "The New Spring,"

---

*See vol. xii. pp. 7–20 for Einleitung zu Kahldorf über den
Adel in Briefen an den Grafen M. von Moltke (1831).—Tr.

dedicated to his sister Charlotte—Heine left
Hamburg and reached Paris at the end of July.

The reasons for his emigration were described
in his " Confessions " in the following humorous
way :

" I had done much and borne much, and when
the sun of the Revolution of July arose in France
I had become absolutely worn out and needed
recreation. Moreover the atmosphere of home
had become day by day more and more unhealthy
for me and I had to consider seriously a change
of climate. I had visions. The clouds frightened me and made all sorts of ominous grimaces
at me. Often methought the sun was a Prussian
cockade ; I dreamed o' nights of an ugly black
vulture that devoured my liver and I became
very melancholy. Besides, I had made the
acquaintance of an old Berlin justice of the peace
who had passed many years in the fortress of
Spandau and who told me how very unpleasant
it was when one had to wear the irons in winter.
In fact I thought it extremely unchristian that
they did not warm the poor fellows' fetters a
little. If they would only warm our chains a bit,
these would not make such a disagreeable

impression, and then even shivery persons could
wear them fairly well; besides, they ought to
have the forethought to perfume the chains with
extract of roses and laurels, as they do in this
country. I asked my justice of the peace if they
often gave him oysters for dinner at Spandau.
He said no ; Spandau was too far from the ocean.
Meat too, he said, was rather uncommon there,
and as to game on wings, there was nothing but
the flies that fell into one's soup. At the same
period I formed the acquaintance of a French
commis voyageur, who was traveling for a wine
business and who could not boast enough of the
jollity of life in Paris at present—how the skies
were hung with fiddles and how from morn till
eve people sang the 'Marseillaise' and 'En
Avant Marchons' and 'Lafayette aux Cheveux
Blancs,' and how Liberty, Equality and Fraternity were written up at all the street corners.
At the same time he praised the champagne sold
by his house and gave me a large number of
copies of their card, and promised to let me have
letters of recommendation to the best restaurants
of Paris in case I wished to visit the capital for
my own enjoyment. Now as I really needed

something to enliven me, and Spandau is too far from the ocean to eat oysters there, and the wild-fowl soup of Spandau did not particularly allure me, and besides, the Prussian chains are exceeding cold in winter and could not well be of use to my health—I resolved to journey to Paris and in the native land of champagne and the 'Marseillaise' to drink the former and listen to the singing of the latter, not to speak of 'En Avant Marchons' and 'Lafayette aux Cheveux Blancs!'*"

Before his departure to Paris Heinrich lived with his mother on the Neuenwall, No. 28, and as he in no wise intended to take up his permanent abode in France, he left his correspondence with finished and unfinished manuscripts at his mother's. In 1833 fire broke out in this place and all his papers went up in smoke. Unfortunately the letters sent to his mother and sister during the Italian voyage and the first years of his residence in Paris were burned at the same time. All the letters in which mention was made of Ludwig Robert, M. Moser and Julius Campe were then destroyed by fire, and Heine lamented in various letters—July 16, 1833 to Varnhagen and

* See vol. viii. pp. 29-30.—TR.

March 7, 1837 to Julius Campe—what a loss of
manuscripts he had sustained through the fire in
his mother's dwelling.

Paris—beautiful, great, elegant, unprejudiced
Eldorado, with her theatres, balls and uncon-
cealed enjoyments, made an intoxicating impression on Heine. Supplied with good introductions,
Heine soon became acquainted with the most
prominent political and literary magnates in the
salons of elegant society. Not merely giving
himself up to the whirl of pleasures, but also observing everything, Heine described the new
impressions with a joyous and humorous pen in
articles for the newspapers and in letters. He
wrote how Paris entranced him by the gayety
which appeared in all social phenomena, and
how the courteous, kindly, polite manners of the
Parisian people pleased him.

"Sweet perfume of politeness, how you did
refresh and restore my wretched soul, which in
Germany had been forced to swallow so much to-
bacco fumes, sauerkraut smell and brutality!
But beside politeness the speech of the French
folk has for me a certain tinge of good breeding;
and any Parisian *dame de la halle* speaks more at-

tractively than a German abbess with sixty-four ancestors."

In the publisher's shop of Heideloff & Campe on the Rue Vivienne Heine was to be found daily; this was a place of meeting for all the more prominent Germans who visited Paris as travelers or had chosen for that city their abode. Felix Mendelssohn, Michael Beer, Koreff, Alexander von Humboldt, Baron Maltitz and many more made the shop their place of tryst in order to swap with each other news from home.

Above all things the splendid galleries of the Louvre riveted Heine's attention, as well as the great annual exhibitions of paintings; and his reports on the latter, in the first part of the " Salon" which appeared in 1833, belong to his best work in the field of the fine arts because of the really plastic descriptions he gave of individual pictures.

Heine's political reports for the *Augsburger Allgemeine Zeitung*, badly mauled by the censorship in Germany, appeared later in the original form under the title, "Condition of France,"* and in this the unsparing and extraordinarily bold statements of the preface threw a strong light on

* See vols, ix. and x. for " Französische Zustände."—TR,

the oppression and fettering of the German press.

The goadings of the censorship and a small difference of opinion with his publisher in that regard had so attacked his exceedingly irritable nerves that Heine had to seek relief at the baths and later, having quite restored his strength, he wrote:

XX

PARIS, October 25, 1833.

DEAR, KIND MOTHER:

I have been back here eight days from Boulogne, where I was for the last six weeks very comfortable, well and jolly. Bathing certainly did me no harm, but still not so much good as formerly. I do not feel myself strengthened by it as before in body and mind, and so must look about for another remedy.

To you, dear Lotta, heartiest thanks for the letters from your chicks; tell Marie and Ludwig that I shall answer them myself as soon as I have time.

A kiss to your youngest. To be hoped you are well—think of you constantly—you can

hardly imagine how much I love you, dear Lotta.
Yesterday I saw a young woman who looked exactly as you did before you were married.   Christiani and wife are not back yet from Bordeaux.

Your wailings, dear mother, over the extraordinary *malheur* not to have sight of me must be
stopped.   To come here into France is not to be
thought of ; give it up or else be assured that
I shall travel to Egypt, whither I have long
cherished a great desire to journey.   If it is not
possible for you to do without my winsome sight,
you know that I am not a disobedient son and
that I will fulfill every one of your wishes if it is
not inconsistent with your own welfare.   I cannot and will not allow you to travel by sea—not
by any means, otherwise I am off to Egypt !   But
if you insist upon it, I will come this summer to
Hamburg for eight days, to that disgraceful lair
where I shall give my enemies the triumph of
seeing me again and being able to heap insults
upon me.

I do not really believe that I shall expose myself to any danger owing to my political position.
But caution is advisable in all things.   You
must not let a soul beside Lotta suspect that I so

much as cherish the idea of coming to Hamburg; otherwise I shall put my enemies even now on guard. But if I come unexpectedly they will have no time to take counsel and come to Hamburg. You will presently learn how much the Prussians are on the watch for me; between ourselves perhaps I exaggerate the matter; but still I am careful, and just because I do take great precautions you can always be without anxiety on my account.

I am safe in all places, am without passions and quiet—and am growing a big stomach like Burgmüller.*

Counsel comes with time. At present my circumstances are so muddy that I cannot determine what I shall do within a six weeks. Mayhap many a thing in this world will change during that time, and I myself meanwhile may obtain at least time and opportunity to consider quietly such a matter as a journey to you. So wait a little; don't make my head spin. I have a lot in my noddle.

I had retained my rooms in town, where for a

* Composer and his sister Charlotte's music teacher in Düsseldorf.

year I enjoyed the greatest quiet, and then, unhappy one! as I returned a family moved in below me with a frightful row and screaming of children!

Farewell; tell me what Max has to say. I have great works in my head, if I could only obtain quiet. God knows, I would make but little row if I were not always forced to make it.

Write to me, dear Lotta. Talk sense into mother. Only write me exactly how mother, you and the children are.

H. HEINE.

Heine's brothers had also left Hamburg. Gustav, born in 1803, had entered the Austrian army after he had first tried farming and then mercantile pursuits; he had risen in the cavalry to first lieutenant. After his marriage with Emma Cahn, who bore him three sons and two daughters, he left the service, founded in Vienna, beginning very modestly, the later official and widely read *Fremdenblatt*, was raised to the nobility, and died in Vienna, November 15, 1886 as a millionaire several times over.

Max, born in 1805, after finishing his medical

studies, entered the civil service of Russia, took part in the Russian campaign in the Caucasus as an army doctor, became physician to the Institute of Cadets, received a title, became court counselor, and left the service with the title of counselor of state after his marriage with the widow of the imperial physician, Privy Councilor von Arndt. He was known as the author of several medical works : " Medical-Topographical Sketch of St. Petersburg," 1844; " History of the Oriental Pest," 1846; " Fragments from the History of Medicine in Russia," 1848; " Items of Medical History from Russia," 1851 ; "Letters of Travel of a Physician," 1853. He was the author of several literary works: "Sketch of Gretsch "; " The Wonders of Lake Ladoga "; " Pictures from Turkey"; " Letters from St. Petersburg "; " Poems "; and " Reminiscences of Heinrich Heine and His Family," 1868. He died in Berlin the sixth of November 1879.

The many worriments of the German censorship, together with the resolutions passed by the German Bundestag, which proscribed not only all of Heine's existing works, but those which he might write in future, raised a bar against his activity as a writer. As early as 1832 he had caused a few articles to be tucked into the *Revue des deux Mondes,* which received much applause, and in consequence he resolved to translate all his earlier works into French. Each of his books as it appeared excited in an ascending degree of fervor an undreamed of recognition and appreciation in the French nation.

A serious evil for Heine were the political refugees who at that time overflowed Paris and toward whose theories of destruction he held himself averse. These men in collusion with the Paris correspondents of German papers cast suspicion on his character by lying gossip. It hurt him sorely that even Börne joined this movement and permitted himself to make sharp attacks on Heine in his letters from Paris, as well as in the *Réformateur,* and accused him of cowardly tacking between the parties and an ambiguous diplomacy. In his letters to various friends he poured out his bitterness over this unfair insult, adding that he was not willing to sacrifice his activity as an author to a newspaper quarrel which would absorb his time and should therefore for the moment remain silent.

After the " Condition of France," the second
part of his " History of Literature," and the
second, third and fourth parts of the " Salon " had
appeared, he published in 1840 his book on Börne.*
With the years his rancor about Börne's conduct had kept on growing, because the latter's
early attacks had found a willing echo among
his enviers and foes, and at last the long announced work appeared. Meantime Börne had
died and to the taunt of the latter's friends that
Heine had not published it while Börne was
alive Heine replied: " Then people would have
said of me that my book had killed him and I
had worried him to death."

Mrs. Wohl, the friend of Börne concerning
whom Heine had made various remarks which
wounded her sadly, caused her friends to put
together a peculiar little volume in which were
collected and published all the hateful utterances Börne had made concerning Heine in private letters addressed to her. A year had gone
by; Heine had quite forgot the matter, when a
certain Mr. Salomon Strauss introduced himself

* See vol. xi. pp. 163–301, " Heinrich Heine über Ludwig
Börne."—Tr.

as the husband of the injured lady and demanded of Heine a public apology or satisfaction by way of arms.

The duel took place ; Heine received a grazing bullet which slightly cut his hip—and therewith was honor satisfied ! But for many years Frankfort was the source of numberless paragraphs which cast scandal on his private life and found acceptance in German and French papers.

The dragging of utterances of the confessional into the question was all the more painful to Heine because people made the accusation that the change of religion which he undertook was not in accordance with his inner persuasion. His entrance into the evangelical (Lutheran) religion had everything to do with the purpose of settling in Hamburg as a lawyer, a profession which at that time was open in Germany only to members of the Christian Church.   Therefore it was that he wrote to Moser: "It can move me but little that they drag the poet from his pedestal, but that they strike so hard, or it were better to say, cudgel away so hard at my private life is extremely vexatious.   As long as I remained a Jew

people called me a Greek of Hellas—and
scarcely am I baptized when I am scouted as a
Jew "! *

But his book on Börne was to exert a still
greater influence on his future; for Heine, who
had entered into a relationship with a beautiful,
lively girl and shared his lodgings with her,
desired to secure her future at all hazards prior to
the duel, not knowing how it might turn out,
and so he caused himself to be legally united to
her. The blessing on their union was given in
the church of St. Sulpice and a legitimate bond
now connected him with a warmly loved companion for many years of his life.

Concerning this step his sister received the
following:

* Heine dubbed his enemy Ludwig Börne a Nazarene and explained his views of Jew and Christian as follows ("H. Heine über
L. Börne," 1840) : " I say Nazarene in order to use neither 'Jewish'
nor 'Christian,' although both expressions are synonymous to
me and are never used by me to denote a faith, but an individuality.
'Jews' and 'Christians' are words that have quite the same
sense in contrast to 'Hellenes,' with which I likewise denote no
special people, but a bent of mind and point of view of certain
men, born and cultivated in them. In this connection I wish to
say : All men are either Jews or Hellenes, namely : persons with
ascetic, iconoclastic, spiritualizing impulses, or, persons with a
realistic nature, glad with life and proud of development."—TR.

XXI

PARIS, September 13, 1841.

DEAR AND MUCH BELOVED SISTER:

Only to-day am I able to officially announce to you my marriage. On August 31 I wedded Mathilde Creszentia Mirat, with whom I have been quarreling every day for more than six years. However she has the noblest and purest heart, is as good as an angel, and her conduct during the many years of our life in common so unblemished that all friends and acquaintances have boasted of her as a model of propriety. * * * * *

H. HEINE.

Heine wrote to his friend Lewald on the announcement of the marriage: "This marital duel which shall never end until one of us is killed is certainly more perilous than the brief visit to the field of honor with Salomon Strauss from the Judengasse of Frankfort."

XXII

PARIS, March 8, 1842.

DEAR, KIND MOTHER:

I trust that these lines reach you in the best of health; with much impatience I await news

MATHILDE MIRAT, HEINE'S WIFE.

from you—how you are, how Lotta is, and
generally how things progress in the family.
Affairs with me are a little better of late; my
eyes are quite restored again, and it is only my
facial paralysis that remains, and that is by no
means painful. Unfortunately my wife has
been ill for ten days and only at this moment
has she dared to go out again. Moreover it
has been frightfully cold, and that has not yet
entirely left us. I live a quiet life, well reasoned
out and hopeful. Nothing new has occurred,
thank God! I already belong to the people who
are satisfied if things remain as of yore. Every
change and noise are distasteful—you can
see by that I have grown old. For the last six
months I have felt a frightful weariness of spirit
and as the hundred-year-old Veronica remarked:
"My thoughts grow less." But this is a passing condition—I know that well enough—
the sequence of great emotion, since unfortunately for the last eight years I have passed
the time in an impassioned state of mind.

Thank God, my wife conducts herself extremely
well. She is a thoroughly square, honest, kind
creature, without falseness or malice. Unfor-

tunately her temperament is very boisterous, her whims never the same and often she is more irritating to me than soothing. I am still bound to her with my whole soul. She is ever my most inward necessity of life—but even that will end some time and I look forward to this period with horror. Then I shall feel only the burden of her whims without the sympathy that makes them easier to bear. At other times anxiety for the helplessness and lack of judgment of my wife worries me in case I die, for she is as inexperienced and without judgment as a three-year-old child! You see, dear mother, how my troubles are at bottom merely the whimsies of a hypochondriac, for the most part!

For the spring I have already made my resolves; I am going into the country in the neighborhood of Paris and not to the baths. Although my finances are somewhat in order, this move will be more agreeable to them than travel. The journey to the Pyrenees and the bad luck that came about the same time ruined me for a time and I had difficulty in getting into the grooves again.

And now farewell, and greet Lotta and her

kittens. Daily I speak of you to my wife, who would so much like to see all of you.

I send kisses to the bridal couple; what date is fixed for the wedding?

My seton in the neck does me good and hurts hardly at all.

Your obedient son,

H. HEINE.

On the night of the fourth of May 1842 the great fire broke out in Hamburg which laid half the city in ashes and also burnt the house of the poet's mother. Notwithstanding the unhappy experience of 1833 Heine had sent her for the second time for safe keeping a chest full of manuscripts and letters, since he thought them safer there than in his own abode, which was often changed. His mother lived on the Neuenwall, which became the prey of the flames, and in the course of this catastrophe the poor poet's papers, his intellectual treasures, went up in smoke; he said himself that they were irreparable. He wrote: "These manuscripts were the product of the first strength of my youth, and I shall never be able to write them down again as they stood,

I wanted to let them lie in order to draw later from
the accumulated capital in my old days when the
freshness of my mind shall have worn off owing
to weakened health."

Heine's sister Charlotte tried at the risk of her
own life to penetrate her mother's abandoned
house in order to save his papers. She was able
to reach the street with a parcel of manuscripts;
but there the situation had swiftly changed. Fire
from the houses opposite sent a rain of sparks and
ashes down on her and thick smoke-clouds darkened her senses with a choking vapor. Pushed
forward by the escaping throng, she kept a des-
perate hold on the papers in her hands, which
however fell to the ground at a sudden push.
Then her senses failed and she would have been
lost had not some person unknown been merciful
enough to drag her out of danger.

XXIII

PARIS, May 13, 1842.

DEAR, KIND MOTHER AND DEAR SISTER:

Yesterday evening I received your letter of the
7th and at least have been able on its account to

sleep quietly through the night.   For twenty-four
hours I have been going about headless, since I
learned the alarming news from the papers.   I
am lost in wonder at you, dear Lotta!   How you
could write so quietly and sensibly—at the sight
of that frightful conflagration.   I thank you from
my heart for setting me at rest as you have.

My wife is sick from fright since she learned
the fearful news.   I hope that the scare and
agitation did not upset you afterward.   My
poor, kind mother!   Do not agitate yourself too
much from sorrow at material losses.

God is a good man.   This time however he
has trusted too much to the good fire establish-
ments of Hamburg.

Farewell ; I send friendly greeting to my
brother-in-law.   I hope to get a good mail to-day.

Your faithful

H. HEINE.

XXIV

PARIS, May 17, 1842.

DEAREST MOTHER AND DEAR SISTER;

I have your letter of the ninth all right and
thank God that we got off with a black eye as

we did. It is certainly a sorrowful thing that
dear mother's house is burned, but the main
point for us is this: your house, dear Lotta, was
untouched. I hope that in another way also
you have not lost much by the mishap; I therefore feel at rest on a matter which from the first
was my chief care. Your husband is of an energetic, practical character and he will replace small
losses soon through his newly stimulated in-
dustry. Did mother have her things insured,
and will the companies pay? Give me some
news in this respect also. I am still as it were
deafened by the whole cursed business; the
nerves of my head were suddenly shaken and
perhaps it will be to-morrow or day after before
my brain clears.

While people were asking me from all sides
for news from Hamburg last Friday I showed
a friend your letter of the 7th, and this man
thought it extremely touching that my poor
mother thought of prepaying the letter for me,
although everything was then in flames. Verily
it is not my fault that this item has come to be
published, as you will see by the inclosed cutting
from the *Nationale*, and several important

journals have already given the incident. My poor, kind mother, who wants to spare me the cost of a few sous while the fire is before your door! Now at any rate she will not prepay the postage any more, just out of spite!

And now farewell and keep me in affection. Kisses to the children. Write me often and much. My wife asks to be heartily remembered. She was very much overwhelmed at the news from Hamburg; she has a very weak head, but a most excellent heart. That Campe was insured and is paid his insurance is very important to me. Have written him to-day.

Your faithful

H. HEINE.

XXV

Monsieur Mr. Henri Heine,
> *agent de change*
>> *à Hambourg.*

PARIS, May 16, 1842.*

MY DEAR UNCLE:

I hope that the affrights of the horrible mishap which has struck Hamburg have not made

---

* Mrs. Anna Hanau, formerly Miss Oswalt of Frankfort-on-the-Main, a friend of Henry Heine, owns the original.

you ill. I can easily imagine how great is the
upset to your nerves, since even at this distance
I felt it myself; to the present hour I have had
a singular stunned feeling in my head. For
twenty-four hours I was without news of any
kind concerning you, when at last I received a
letter from my dear mother and sister. Lotta
wrote with a sense and a quiet worthy of a field
marshal. Here in Paris the misfortune made a
great sensation and met with a sympathy which
is truly cause for shame to those Hamburg people
who are not healed of their hatred of the French,
but continue to show the same down to the
present. The French are the squarest of people.

So then, notwithstanding the excellent fire
engine plant of which you have always boasted,
you are half burned to the ground! What a
stretch between the Deichstrasse and Uncle
Heine's on the Jungfernstieg! The Jungfernstieg burnt down along with the pavilions!
I am very desirous to learn how far the insurance
companies will fulfill their obligations.

Farewell, dear uncle, and greet Aunt Jette
heartily from me; she must have been not a
little anxious; and also Hermann and the young

ladies. My wife, who is in the country for her health at this moment, came in weeping that day when she heard of the misfortune; for the rest she is in fair health. The catastrophe on the Versailles railway also shook us a good deal, because many of our friends were destroyed by it. What wretchedness!

Your faithful nephew,
H. HEINE.

Concerning the great Hamburg conflagration Heine wrote on occasion : " Poor old Hamburg is a wreck, and the spots I knew so well, which are so intimately bound up with all the reminiscences of my youth are now a smoking ash heap ! I deplore most the loss of that old St. Peter's tower—it was so lifted up and superior above the pettinesses of its surroundings! The city will soon be built up again—my old crook-cornered, slab-sided Hamburg! The big gabled house where my cobbler lived, and where I devoured oysters alongside the flaunting—a prey to the flames! The *Hamburger Correspondenz* it is true reports that the "Dirtwall" will soon arise like a phenix from the ashes—but alas, it will

never be the same old *Dreckwall* again! And
the town hall—how often I stood entranced before the paintings of emperors which, as if carved
out of Hamburg smoked beef, ornamented its
façade! Are all the magnificent and finely
powdered bigwigs saved which gave to the heads
of the republic there a majestic appearance?
Heaven forefend that at such a moment as this I
should tweak ever so little at those old wigs!
On the contrary I would rather bear witness on
this occasion that in Hamburg the government
always surpassed the governed in good will
toward social progress. The people always stood
on a lower level than their representatives, among
whom were men of the most remarkable culture
and wisdom. But it is to be hoped that the
great conflagration will have somewhat enlightened the baser intellects and that the entire
population of Hamburg now perceives that the
spirit of the age, which did them a kindness by
means of their misfortune, must not hereafter
be insulted by a wretched shopman's wisdom.
More especially, equality in citizenship for men
of different religious views * can certainly not

* This took place at last in 1849.

be postponed in Hamburg any longer. Let us expect the best from the future ; Heaven does not send great trials for nothing.

XXVI

PARIS, June 23, 1842.
DEAR, KIND SISTER :

I have still to thank you for your dear, dainty and clever letters.

You are a splendid person in all ways—you know I rarely indulge in compliments—but you, dear Lotta, deserve a whole cargo of flattering words. Write often to me ; you have no idea how you make me gay and refreshed. You write charmingly. I am curious whether your eldest daughter follows your footsteps. Has she by any chance the gentleness of her grandmother?

My wife sends her regards. She will please you when you see her. A thoroughly honest, angelically kind creature, generous and noble-minded through and through, but full of moods and uncontrolled ; at times tormenting and a scold—things which are always bearable, however, since with them all she remains very pretty and graceful.

Latterly I saw young Holländer, who carries back greetings to you ; he does not look at all changed with years.

Regards to my brother-in-law. I kiss heartily the little puppets. More presently !

I am trying the water cure now—whether it will help me God only knows !

Your true brother,
H. HEINE.

XXVII

PARIS, August 10, 1842.

DEAREST LOTTA :

I am about to journey to the baths and to-day am too much occupied with preparations to write you a long letter, as I would like to do and as you indeed deserve. Your last letter was so delightfully kind it gave me great pleasure. The other day Armand Heine * was here, whom I had never met and who was able to tell me a good deal about Hamburg. To my delight he told me that your children had come out well,

---

* Armand Heine, died 1883, a nephew of the poet, founded with his brother Michael Heine the famous bank of A. & M. Heine in Paris. Michael's daughter Alice, widow of the Duc de Richelieu, married for second husband the Prince of Monaco.

and that your eldest daughter Marie had become as slender and clever as her mother.
She might put her pen to paper some day and
write to her uncle.

I am going to Boulogne-sur-Mer with my wife;
you can write me there *poste restante* if you wish
to please me. My wife is pretty well at present.
We often talk of you and she already knows a
good many of our family music pieces. Moreover
this winter she is to learn German. You see how
I educate her and how she will soon become an
ornament to our family. For some time now she
scolds very little and has become very corpulent.
In other respects she is kindness personified and
wins all hearts.

Greet your husband and kiss the dear children.
And now farewell, and keep in affection

Your trusty brother

H. HEINE.

Mathilde never learned German, and the only
sentence which stuck to her memory was the
standing formula when a German came on a visit:
Guten Tag, mein Herr; nehmen sie Platz! Then
she would break out in a peal of laughter and

run away, leaving the visitor alone in the room, petrified at the singular reception, until he was led into the sick chamber of the poet.

XXVIII

PARIS, November 28, 1842.

DEAREST SISTER :

Although my head is as it were stunned by hard work, I hasten to send you my congratulations.   How shall I express the pleasure which almost overwhelmed me at the coming of your letter?   I and my dear wife—who takes the most perfect interest in you—both of us have passed a very pleasurable hour.   She wishes to be recommended most warmly, and particularly to have you thanked for the portrait which we received. She was beside herself with joy when she got it and since then it is on parade in our drawing room, where it is shown to everybody and is often admired.

Outwardly and intellectually you are still so young—and already you are marrying off a daughter and soon will be a grandmother!   And then old Gluck will be a great-grandmother!

O that at this moment I had poor little father with me! How he would have rejoiced! That is constantly on my mind, and so, happiness makes me sad! Allow me to most obediently commend myself to the bride and to the groom as well. I thank my brother-in-law most heartily for having written me at once and I congratulate him with great joy.

If I could only be with you for a few days! What a sorrow! It is however impossible just now. The news that Marie will come to Paris puts ecstasy into my deepest soul. She will be convinced that she has no commonplace uncle and that her aunt is pretty and kind. I send greeting to mother and embrace you both. As I said, I am much overcome by many labors. I have at the present moment a lot round the ears. Till the end of February I have more than enough to do, affairs of the most important kind, and unfortunately my head is sick and often I have to take a holiday against my will.

But I shall get through and then I shall do something permanent for my headache.

Your faithful brother,
H. HEINE.

The poet had put together his correspondence with the *Allgemeine Zeitung* in the miscellaneous writings under the title of "Lutetia" and brought them out in book form.* It is a historical treatise on the daily happenings in Paris during the reign of Louis Philippe, the period of the citizen kingship, in which politics, fine art and social life are described in a piquant and amusing way. Even at that date Heine was giving warning of the bold rise of socialism to which the future would belong, unless a thorough reformation should be made in existing circumstances. "The propaganda of communism has a language that every people understands. The elements of this universal speech are as simple as hunger can be, as envy, as death itself. It is such an easy language to learn; it will resolve itself into a world-wide revolution—the great duel of those who have nothing with the aristocracy of ownership."

In 1843 Heine published in Laube's *Zeitung für die Elegante Welt* a new humorous epic called the "Midsummer Night's Dream,"† which

---

* See vols. ix. and x. under "Französiche Zustände." For his remarks on Communism see vol. x. p. 110.—TR.

† For "Atta Troll, ein Sommernachtstraum," see vol. ii. pp. 138–210.—TR.

only later, in 1847, on its appearance in book form, obtained from the public a general understanding and recognition.

XXIX

Monsieur Mr. Henri Heine,
agent de change
à Hambourg.

PARIS, February 11, 1843.

DEAR UNCLE:

These are the first lines I have written for three weeks. For the weakness in my eyes had started afresh with the utmost violence and it is only to-day that I feel myself a little relieved. I would not speak to you of my own sufferings, since you have more cause for sorrow than I,* if I did not have to state the reason why you receive a letter from me only at this date. The sorrowful news which has put me in mourning was reported to me by my mother ten days ago, and I can assure you that meantime I have thought

---

* This is a letter of condolence upon the death of the elder Henry Heine's daughter Matilda, in the bloom of her seventeen years. Dr. H. Oswalt of Frankfort, nephew of Henry Heine, has the original.

often of you and not without tears. Heaven
keep you and pour balm on your loving heart.
My wife, who offers you the most sorrowful sympathy, begs to be remembered.

I pray you assure Aunt Jette that at a distance
I felt her sorrows as my own. Remember me to
Emily and Hermann, who was always a good
boy.

I can never tell you, dear uncle, how crushed
my heart is to think that when such mournful
events happen I cannot even come to Hamburg!
But since I have been married I am not so
movable as formerly. I cannot leave my wife
here [in Paris] alone, and it costs too much money
and trouble to take her with me. For the rest I
pass here a happy domestic life, enjoy the most
valuable quiet of spirits, and need nothing but re-
lease from my eye trouble and the vile headaches
in which that trouble has its real root. Latterly
I have had a seton put in the back of my neck
and hope to obtain some soothing of the pain.
Inside me, as I say, I am thoroughly well and eat
as much as six Frenchmen—yes, almost as much
as three Hamburgers.

And now, my dear uncle, farewell; happier

hours will be sure to return. I love you much.

Your obedient nephew,

H. HEINE.

XXX

PARIS, February 21, 1843.

DEAR, KIND MOTHER:

My dawdling in writing you must pardon. Unfortunately my eye troubles were to blame for my not writing for some time. I have been able to see at all only for the last ten days. This temporary burden has worried me on this occasion very much, because it was accompanied by a weakening of the face muscles on the right side (from the crown of the head to the chin). Still my eye trouble seems to have been only a passing ill which at certain times is likely to make its appearance and disappear just as regularly; the facial paralysis (which, thank God, is not visible) remaining behind will take somewhat longer to drive off. For that purpose I have had a seton placed in the back of the neck. Otherwise I am healthy from my heart outward; indeed I am in better case than ever before.

My trouble interferes with my work a great deal, because I am sparing myself in an extraordinary fashion. I have a good constitution of body and hope to skip about in this world for a long time to come.

But that you, dear mother, have been ill wor-ries me not seldom; write to me soon and at length. Hearty and many greetings to Lotta! I think of her very often. Mme. Holländer said delightful things to me about my niece Marie. How young Mrs. Holländer remains, and, in spite of her twenty years in Hamburg, has not lost in the slightest degree her French charm! I saw her yesterday at a ball at her father's, old Worms, whither I went, be it said in parenthesis, only on account of my wife. She so loves to dance, and she deserves that I should sacrifice myself for her now and then! More-over in these later years she has taken ex-cellent care of me and on this side I am a happy man.

You ask me about "Atta Troll"; he may have received a little warm color from a Jewish Emancipationist—but between ourselves I only had in mind a satire on the ideas of liberalism entertained by mankind. You see that I answer your questioning.

And now, dear mother, farewell, and write much to me and often.

Your faithful son,

H. HEINE.

XXXI

PARIS, March 22, 1843.

DEAREST MOTHER:

If you weigh my every word on goldsmith's balances I cannot write to you any more with the unconsciousness and easy hurry I have hitherto employed. It should rather be a reason for quiet to your mind that I do report everything to you, even a fit of bad temper that has no cause.

When I wrote you last, two corpses lay in my house; two neighbors had died of typhus fever, one of them a young man of thirty-one, who left his wife and children helpless. My wife lay sick and the weather was very cold. Under such circumstances one does not write joyous letters. To-day it is wondrous fine; for the last eight days we've been getting weather like spring;

I feel myself uncommonly inspirited and well;
moreover I am able to write once more. My
wife is restored to health too, and, thank God,
scolds away in full possession of health. I hope
now that you also are entirely on your legs again.

Farewell, and remember me to dear Lotta and
the children.

Your faithful son,

H. HEINE.

XXXII

PARIS, April 8, 1843.

DEAREST SISTER :

Mother wrote me the other day that the
wedding takes place the eighth of this month.
That's to-day; and I am steadily thinking about
you all. I wait impatiently for news from you,
whether everything went off nicely. You must
have your hands full to-day. Since the ever-to-
be-remembered day at the Zollenspiker * you
have had no such important day. I congratulate you and embrace you from my heart ; I beg
also that you will assure the young couple of my

* Place at Vierlanden near Hamburg where marriages are celebrated.

most profound sympathy and love. The jolliest congratulations to your husband and many friendly remembrances. Kiss mother for me, old Gluck and your chicks. My wife sends you the happiest and most loving messages. I hope that you are in good health.

We are getting on well, except that my poor head is no better. * * * * *

H. HEINE.

XXXIII

PARIS, May 23, 1843.

DEAREST MOTHER:

I received your letter of the ninth of May all right and saw therein that you were well. Your letter of the same date last year was less delightful!

I can never forget the terror of that conflagration. And I also never forget how great my dear sister's behavior was on that occasion! What a heroine! Wellington * is a dishrag to her!

I send my hearty greeting to Lotta, and thank her for her latest report on the marriage of my niece. She must have received my congratulations at the same time. But now I

* For Heine's estimate of the English military idol see vol. vi, p. 291.—TR.

would like to know how matters stand with the young couple. May the honeymoon never contrast too sharply with the months that come after!

Nothing has changed in my case in wedlock; on the contrary, each year my wife gets more sensible and docile, and I have not yet regretted my marriage. That's a good deal to say in the present generation and in Paris, where bad marriages swarm; good ones are so rare that they ought to be preserved in alcohol.

My head trouble is always the same thing. I don't know yet what kind of a cure I shall try this summer; traveling expenses are too great, since I have to take my wife with me ; can't leave her in Paris alone. Anyhow I shan't travel at all. Perhaps I'll take a house in the neighborhood of Paris where there is some country air, if it can be cheaply put in order.

You have no conception how very often I think of you. Only write me often and much, how you feel, how things are with you.

As soon as you get a letter from Max let me know. I would like to know whether he received the letter which I sent him lately by way of Riga to a friend who agreed to forward it to his address at St. Petersburg, which I did not know.

And now farewell; kiss Lotta and the dear children for me.

Your faithful son,

H. HEINE.

XXXIV

PARIS, June 18, 1843.

DEAREST, KIND MOTHER:

Your welcome letter of the 5th instant I received last week all right together with the inclosures, and I thank you for the evidences of your warm motherly love which assert themselves on this as on all other occasions.

Since there are so many wretches in the world; since I am always very ungratefully treated for the many good acts I do; since in general many a thing to put me out of sorts weighs upon me, it is certainly a great comfort for me to have so nice a mother as you are, and on that account alone your loving care for me is even now of the greatest value.

I don't know yet to whom I can give the papers to keep. I think it is best if I keep them

myself. For I am sound and well from my in-
most heart, and my headaches are of the kind
that lets one become old and gray. In any case
I live so moderately that my health will rather
improve than worsen. Therefore quiet yourself.
I hope that you too, dear mother, are in good
health. Do write to me on this point how you
are getting on. May Heaven keep us all! Write
me how everything is where you are.

As I do not read *Der Telegraph*,* don't forget
to keep your eye on it for me. Uncle has sent
me his likeness with a loving letter ; the portrait †
is wonderfully like. Carl also wrote me very
warmly, so that I am now, thank God, in the best
of understanding with the family. I think Max
would do better if he sent his letters for me

---

* *Der Telegraph*, a newspaper edited by Carl Gutzkow, one of
Heine's chief enemies.

† A lithographic likeness of Salomon Heine by Otto Spekter in
Hamburg.

Salomon Heine was born October 19, 1767, died December 23,
1844, married to Betty Goldschmidt (born 1777, died 1837). Their
six children and sons-in-law are all dead : Friederike, married to
Moritz Oppenheimer. Fanny, married to Schröder, M. D.
Hermann, born 1804, died unmarried at Rome in 1830. Amalie,
married John Friedländer. Carl, born 1810, died 1865, married
to Cecilie Furtado in Paris. Therese, died 1880 in Ottensen,
married to Dr. Adolf Halle.

through you at Hamburg; I believe the post direct this way from St. Petersburg is not very sure.

Write me how matters stand with Lotta and the young bridal couple. I think of staying in Paris till the fourth of next month and then going for six weeks or two months to a seaside resort, perhaps to Boulogne again. The quiet, sea air and also the baths there will be wholesome for me.

It looks very badly for my literary work in German because of the botherations by the censorship. If you write at once I shall catch your letter here in Paris. My wife sends you a kiss.

Your faithful son,

H. HEINE.

XXXV

TROUVILLE, August 5, 1843.

DEAREST, KIND MOTHER:

During three weeks I dragged myself about with an utter irresolution as to whither I should go. Finally I came here, where I have been for eight days, just as irresolute whether to stay or not. That is the reason I did not write to you earlier. But now that I am determined

to hold on here a good while, I report my good
health to you and beg that you will inform me
as to yours as soon as possible. My address is
*H. Heine à Trouville, département Calvados en
France.* Write me very soon how you are all
getting on. I and my dear wife are well,
and this year the sea baths agree with me
very well. Constantly we speak of you;
and you cannot conceive how eagerly my wife
desires to see you, for I often tell her how
much love you have always shown me and how
there are few mothers like you in the world.

Unhappily my eyes are very weak, as always in
summer. Kiss Lotta and the chicks. Good-by,
old Gluck!

Your most profoundly affectionate son,

H. HEINE.

I beg you not to frank your letters.

XXXVI

PARIS, September 18, 1843.

DEAR KIND, DEAR MOTHER:

Your letter of August 18 which you addressed to Trouville was duly forwarded, and

since then I have also received your letter of September 2. With deep sorrow I perceive from
the latter that Uncle Heine's health looks badly;
I pray you always write me exactly and exhaust-
ively how he gets on. In this respect I am, if
not entirely at rest, still possessed of the firm be-
lief that the health of this dear man has an iron
foundation, which perhaps might be slowly worn
away by constant shocks, but will last for a long
time to come for the happiness of all. Except
for excess at meals, uncle has never broken a rule
of good health, and the genuine life springs have
only been attacked now and then by sorrow—God
preserve him!

And you, sweet old cat, how are you getting on?
If you die before I can see you again I shall put
a bullet through my head. Mark that against
the chance that any suggestion should assail
you to exchange your house on the Dammthor
for a less excellent lodging. Mark that, will
you? and then you will not commit any such
folly!

I spoke to a friend of Max yesterday, Gretsch
from Petersburg, who knows you too and spoke
of you with so much reverence and respectful

affection that I roamed about all day very melancholy and with my heart cooked soft.

If it were possible (but at the present moment
it is almost impossible) I would visit you this
year; but in any case it shall be next year.
Greet Lotta and the children.

As I hear, X.* is to be in Paris.   What happiness for Paris—a reparation for the failure of the
Queen of England to come here!

Farewell.   In fine, stay alive as long as possible
and take you note of what I have said.

Your faithful son,

H. HEINE.

XXXVII

PARIS, September 21, 1843.

DEAREST SISTER:

You will receive these lines by the hand of
Mlle. A. de C., a young person who is as remarkable for character as she is black of complexion.
She is of African race, but educated in Paris from
her tenderest infancy, and in truth in the same
boarding school where my wife passed several

* A frequenter of his uncle Salomon's table, whose overweening
conceit often roused Heine's ridicul

years. She is the latter's most intimate friend and you may judge from that if I know her well and if I can recommend her to you with as good a conscience as hearty warmth.

Her father is a rich merchant from St. Thomas; latterly he married a rich Hamburg woman and is now in that city; in order to arrange delicate affairs with him Mlle. de C. goes to Hamburg in company with her brother, a young man as black as he is good.

Receive them with kindness for our sakes: your sister-in-law also begs you to do so. If you can assist them in any way with good counsel and help, you will be sure to do it. The point is to bring a pressure to bear on her father; she will not wish to acknowledge this at once, because she is of an uncommonly high-spirited nature; but the young man will soon instruct you as to their circumstances. I have also recommended her to Cecilie Heine.

I get no letter from you and we are therefore living in the greatest anxiety. Greet your husband and kiss the children for me.

I embrace you heartily.

Your faithful brother,

H. HEINE.

You are so quick and have such a kind heart that I do not doubt you will be of the happiest usefulness to our young friend.

XXXVIII

PARIS, October 18, 1843.

DEAR, KIND, PRECIOUS MOTHER:

I got your last letter all right, and your idea to appoint a rendezvous with Max in Hamburg in spring has roused powerfully in me the desire to see you again. But I want to see you sooner than spring—this very year in fact —and before you know where you are I shall be standing before you as large as life!

But that is a great, big secret and you must not tell a soul a word of it; for I am not traveling by water, but straight through Germany; and as I speak of it to no one here and moreover shall journey quickly, there is nothing to fear from the government. But as I said, not a word of this to a soul! I shall write to Uncle Heine, but only the day before I leave—not earlier than that, for weighty reasons.

If Lotta can keep silent, you may let her know about it. I leave my wife here in Paris at the boarding school where she was formerly. As I do not know when I shall get off, do not write to me at this address.

Next week more from

Your faithful son,

H. HEINE.

XXXIX

PARIS, October 21, 1843.

DEAR, KIND MOTHER:

I hope to find you in the best of health, and to-day shall write you but little, since I shall see you ten or fourteen days hence and then can tell you everything possible that is loving and warm. I am on the point of starting, first to Brussels, whence I shall probably go to Amsterdam, and thence by way of Bremen to Hamburg, where I look with certainty for the best of welcomes from you. I have made up my mind quickly to this journey; things of the kind must not be postponed. That were as unwise as painful!

And so I am soon to see you again, dear

mother. Don't be frightened at my changed appearance. I will write you again on the way.

Kiss Lotta and the children—but I shall soon kiss you all with my own lips!

H. HEINE.

XL

BREMEN, October 28, 1843.

DEAR, KIND MOTHER:

You see my journey is half finished. I arrived here an hour ago sound and well, but very tired. How I am to go forward to Hamburg I do not know yet, since I do not wish to travel through a night again and the post coach only leaves this evening. So perhaps I shall only get to you early day after to-morrow, or if possible to-morrow evening very late.

Kiss Lotta and the children, whom I shall kiss myself day after to-morrow.

Your faithful son,

H. HEINE.

During his journeyings about Germany it was necessary for Heine to take the greatest precautions, because the poet was forbidden to enter the Prussian states * and at the frontiers the most particular orders of arrest lay in waiting for him and were renewed every year.

After an absence of twelve years Heine was driven to Hamburg by the yearning to see his native land once more and to embrace his mother and sister. He passed his six weeks of stay almost exclusively within the narrowest family circle of his dear ones, and was hardly accessible at all for the greater number of his acquaintances there. Besides, he made use of his presence in Hamburg to conclude a contract with his publisher Julius Campe for the issue of his complete works ; and he exacted a royalty on a yearly ascending scale up to the sum of eighteen hundred marks (about seven hundred dollars), which was to pass to his wife for her life after his death. Anxiety for Mathilde's future caused him to close the bargain with a certain precipitation, and afterward he often rued the day when he was so docile with his publisher.

* The reader will remember how singularly intermixed at that period were the various states in Germany ; Prussia especially held outlying portions of Germany hard to evade on a direct route.—TR.

Heine began the return trip in December, and promised to repeat his visit for a longer stay next year, in company with Mathilde, concerning whom he could not say enough in praise. Owing to the setting in of frost he had to run the risk of journeying by land, and it is touching how at each stop Heine caused word to be sent to his mother, who was in the greatest terror on his account.

XLI

HANOVER, December 9, 1843.

DEAREST, KIND MOTHER:

Yesterday I arrived here sound and well. I shall stay a few days on the score of business; I have nothing to fear. The weather is wonderful and just this may perhaps induce me to remain for a special purpose here a few days. I am happy and gay of mood and hope that now you too are not sad.

Kiss and greet Lotta and her children. In about ten days I shall be in Paris and will write you at once.

Your faithful son,

H. HEINE.

XLII

COLOGNE, December 14, 1843.

DEAR, KIND MOTHER:

As you see, I did not stay in Hanover as long as I purposed. Now I'm in Cologne and intend to stay one day. Day after to-morrow I shall go to Brussels by railway, an easy day's journey, and thence it is but a leap to Paris. So the journey is as good as done with and now you can sleep quietly. At this moment I am very tired from the journey by night; otherwise jolly and quite well. The weather was most fine and in this respect Heaven particularly favored me.

And now farewell; I shall not write for eight days. Greet Lotta and kiss the children for me. Also greet heartily my brother-in-law and nephew. Weary and in haste,

Your faithful son,

H. HEINE.

XLIII

BRUSSELS, December 18, 1843.

DEAREST MOTHER:

I have just reached here sound and well. Early to-morrow morning I shall travel toward

Paris, where I shall be day after to-morrow early. So I am as it were at home and this letter may serve now as an announcement to that effect. So be at rest and let me be quiet. Shall not be able to write you again for six or eight days, because as soon as I get to Paris I shall be overwhelmed by such a deluge of business that I can hardly hope to get to writing very soon.

So far I have had wondrous fine weather. Greet Lotta, my dear sister and her children. All my thoughts on the journey traveled from you to my wife and from my wife back to you. May I again find you all well and happy next year—that is my only care.

My pen won't work, but I am ever

Your faithful son,

H. HEINE.

XLIV

PARIS, January 23, 1844.

DEAR, KIND SISTER:

Mother announced the fortunate delivery of your daughter about a fortnight ago, but since then I have been without news of her condition, which is the main point, and for that I have to complain of your neglect. I hope that Marie is in good health and that I shall get news from you pretty soon that will put my mind at rest.

I and my wife are in a fair state of health and constantly talk about you. I cannot tell her enough what a splendid sister you are, and the love with which I speak of you almost makes her jealous. We live quiet and retired.

*   *   *   *   *

My plans for this summer are still the same, and I shall write to you about them in good time. Write to me much and circumstantially, so that I can form an exact estimate of local matters with you. But especially let me always know the exact news concerning the state of uncle's health. I hope that you are feeling well and do not tax yourself too much. Mother complains a little of her state of health; I trust it is nothing.

Despite my increasing paralysis of the face, I work a good deal. But perhaps some day I may have to pitch my pen to the devil and be condemned to do nothing at all!

My wife is conducting herself pretty well; does not scold too often, but always remains a spendthrift.   I get through with difficulty and trouble, but I do get through, and the cares vanish.   If I only could see you now and then, sweet angel, just to look at you without saying a word!

Farewell, and greet the whole gossipred from me—the cock of the house and the chicks.

Your discursive brother,

H. HEINE.

XLV

PARIS, February 20, 1844.

DEAREST MOTHER:

In the letter I wrote Lotta there was nothing at all, and I do not know why Lotta did not want to let you see it.

I can't write you much to-day and perhaps not in the first four weeks either, for my eye trouble has come back again and meantime I must spare my eyes very much.   The physician tells me that this time I must wait longer than ever until the crisis is passed and I can use my eyes again as before.   I greet Lotta and the children. Write soon to your

Faithful son,

H. HEINE.

XLVI

PARIS, March 4, 1844.

DEAR, KIND MOTHER :

You must always believe my word, for I always tell you everything. Your letter came just now and from it I see that you are fabricating for yourself needless ideas and cares. My eyes, or rather the eye from which I suffered, has been healed ; but I have to spare myself, and so I write to no one, read nothing and take care of myself. I hope in a few days I shall be entirely on my feet again. I yearn to see you all again. That shall take place this summer in any case, even though I go again to Hamburg for a short time and leave my wife behind again.

*　　　*　　　*　　　*　　　*

H. HEINE.

XLVII

PARIS, July 11, 1344.

DEAR, KIND SISTER :

Yesterday I wrote to dear mother and announced that I should make the journey to Hamburg *per* land, and in truth by way of Ant-

werp.   So now she will not tremble at every puff
of wind.

But to you, dear Lotta, I will tell the truth,
namely : that next week, the twentieth of July, I
shall leave Havre for Hamburg on the steamer
and therefore get to you on the 22d or 23d.
Mother need know nothing until I have arrived
sound and well with my better half.

It is the finest season for journey by sea and
apart from seasickness there is nothing at all to
worry over.   Now however, dear Lotta, comes
the question of lodging, and on this point I shall
tell you to-day most particularly what is to be
done.

This year I did not go to the seaside and my
nerves are in such an irritated state that I shall
certainly fall sick, if I do not fill my lungs with
fresh air for a time in the country or with sea
air on the coast, and that too in the greatest
quiet of soul.   So if you, dear Lotta, could find
a country dwelling for me near the Dammthor
where I can pass August, September and October, I should be greatly accommodated.   But
if that is not possible, I shall stay at first only a
few days in Hamburg and then go at once with

my wife to Helgoland in order to breathe in sea
air for a few weeks and, in case they do not dis-
agree with me, to take baths also. I am in such
great need of this!

As soon as I arrive in Hamburg I shall drive
to. Hillert's again, although I foresee that his
newly built Stadt London will not be good for
me who have a horror of all new constructions.
But I shall stay there only a few days and then
go to the country, if I get a country abode, or to
Helgoland if I get none. If I go to Helgoland
you can look up meantime a house for me in
town in your neighborhood which I can move
into at once on my return.

In case it does not put you out (but only in
this case) it would be agreeable to me if you
could shelter my wife for the few days I shall pass
at Hillert's, not because I want to save money,
but because it seems to me more respectable for
my wife not to go to a hotel. In any case I shall
write you again on this point.

How would it be if you gave yourself a little
pleasure and accompanied us to Helgoland?
That would be the most pleasing so far as
I am concerned. Could you possibly do that?

In any case it would be very good for your health.

*　　*　　*　　*　　*

As I shall stay there only till the middle or, at farthest, the end of November, I shall bring nothing with me for housekeeping and so must hire the country house or later the town house entirely furnished and supplied with all necessary utensils. But the equipment need not be complete, since I am quite indifferent whether or not I buy there all kinds of things and furnishings which I can always use there later, or perhaps even take away with me. I need two bedchambers with one bed each, one living room, one workroom and a little room for a maid.

*　　*　　*　　*　　*

H. HEINE.

XLVIII

PARIS, July 13, 1844.

MY DEAR LOTTA :

I am up to the neck in preparations for the journey, and, as I wrote you, am departing about this time from Paris and shall be next Saturday morning early on the Hamburg steamer with my wife. In regard to the letter which I wrote you day before yesterday, I remark further that after a careful consultation with my physician, I shall in any case go to the sea baths at Helgoland, and so for the present shall pass but a few days in Hamburg. So I now see that I shall only need a dwelling in Hamburg after I return thither from Helgoland, and therefore you need trouble yourself only for such a house and not for a country place. In any case, in respect of this town house also, you must not hire it until I have seen it; I shall be there so soon. I would like best the Esplanade, but your Theater Strasse somewhat near the Jungfernstieg would be just as good.

Perhaps I shall write to mother again before I leave, but not to tell her that I go by water; I shall only say that she may expect me between the 23rd and the 25th, so that she may not get a scare.

My wife and I are in thoughts already in Hamburg, and we speak of you constantly. How I rejoice to think of seeing you and the children again!

The weather is nice and friendly and cool; I am traveling in the finest season. I pray you make it possible that you and Marie can go with us to Helgoland. The cost of everything is very small and the air is so delicious and healing.

To-day Furtado leaves here for Hamburg in order to take up Cäcilie * there and go with her to the baths of Leuk in Switzerland.

Greet your husband for me and kiss the children for me on account.

How I shall rejoice to see you and my old mother again!

Your brother,
H. HEINE.

On a splendid sunshiny afternoon the Havre steamer came into this port a little late, and we were all hanging about the bridge for a long while in the utmost excitement over the expectation of learning to know Mathilde, Heine's wife. At last the ship approached and my uncle

---

* Cäcilie Furtado, wife of Carl Heine and settled in Paris, known for her wealth and the many beneficent foundations she made in France. Her husband Carl Heine, born January 20, 1810, died at Bagnères de Luchon, July 4, 1865, having been struck by apoplexy while out walking; he was buried in Paris. The marriage was childless and they adopted a little girl. This adoptive child was married to General Ney, Prince of Elchingen, and having become a widow early, married in second nuptials the Duc de Rivoli.

came ashore. He had grown a little stouter, had
nothing external about him that looked sickly,
and had on his arm a stately lady in a simple
gray traveling dress. Mathilde was a really
very beautiful woman of tall figure, somewhat
luxuriant lines and lovely oval face framed with
chestnut hair, red, full lips which showed pretty,
white teeth, and large, expressive eyes which
shot fire when under excitement.

We were destined to see these fine eyes flash
very soon, when, after a joyous greeting, my
father led her to the carriage and handed her a
box after she had entered—but with a start of
pain let it fall as he felt his finger sharply bitten.
A shrill scream escaped from Mathilde, for in
the box was Cocotte the parrot, her darling,
which she had brought from Paris.

" Heavens, what carelessness to scare him so,
after poor Cocotte has just been so seasick ! "
said she in an irritated tone.

But happily Cocotte had sustained no injury,
and smiling joyously the beautiful woman's
features smoothed themselves out. My uncle
approached laughing loudly and said : " Dear
brother-in-law, you nearly forfeited Mathilde's

favor forever; I wrote you that I would come
with my family, that is to say, with my wife and
parrot, and now you ignore the latter entirely
until he has to introduce himself to you with a
bite!"

Cocotte was an uncontrolled, evil-disposed
creature which began to clap his beak and
scream savagely when in a bad humor, a thing
which was extremely irritating to the poor poet
with his many headaches.

One day Mathilde rushed into the room when
Cocotte had an attack of the cramps. "Heine"
she sobbed "Cocotte is dying." And Heine
replied in German, not understood by Mathilde,
"God be praised"; but the prayer came too
early, for the bird returned to health.

During the first days of his stay Heine and his
wife lived in our house in the greater Theater
Strasse, and during the next week moved into an
elegant lodging in a first floor on the Esplanade. Meals were chiefly taken with us, and
Mathilde, who enjoyed very much the dishes
peculiar to Hamburg, soon felt herself very gay
and at home, all the more since we all spoke
French and her sportive ideas got applause.

The first visit which Heine made with his wife was to his uncle Salomon, who took a liking to Mathilde, since Heine, acting the interpreter with great tact, knew how to get round the fact that she did not understand a word of German. The old gentleman was a kindly, beneficent man, but a fearful domestic tyrant and could not bear to have people converse in his presence in a foreign tongue, because he understood German only. And concerning his German Heine said with no little descriptiveness : " At official dinners a servant stood on one side of the table for the dative and at the other side a servant for the accusative." *

One of his sons-in-law, who had settled before in England and had there failed in business, liked to embrace every occasion to speak English; one day he carried on in a loud voice a conversation in English with the wife of the British consul, who sat opposite. The old man, who had taken the lady in, listened quietly for a time ; finally he wrinkled his brow and, inter-

---

* An allusion to the errors commonly made by Germans in using the accusative for the dative case or vice versa ; more particularly the use of *mich* for *mir*.—TR.

rupting the conversation, said: " Is it not so, my
son-in-law speaks good English ?—but I had to
pay for it, for his learning this language cost me
half a million marks ! "

In summer Salomon Heine inhabited a splendid villa at Ottensen, whose flower garden ran
in terraces to the brink of the Elbe, and the
family dinners were given there on Wednesday
and Sunday.

Next Sunday the fashionable carriage of Uncle
Salomon came round for Heine and his wife in
order to take them to the country seat to dine,
and Heine accepted this invitation with ill grace,
because he knew that Mathilde, his gay child of
nature, did not fit in very well with the plutocrats
of the family there assembled.

Aware of the orders of the old gentleman that
no one should converse in a foreign tongue, only
a few French words were whispered on the sly,
and poor Mathilde had to hold her tongue for
two hours and bored herself fearfully. At
dessert the unlucky chance befell that the old
man sent round a bunch of grapes of unusual
size, with berries almost as large as plums,
which was grown in his hothouse, but only as a

curiosity for the amazement of all. When the
plate reached Mathilde she took the bunch,
since she did not think otherwise than that it
was meant for her and she paid those grapes
special attention. After a little the old man
asked in an irritated way where the bunch was,
and when he was told what had occurred, Heine
said with quick resolution : " Dear uncle, your
grape bunch was a miracle, but still another
miracle has occurred—it has disappeared; an
angel carried it off." The old man laughed
and the grapes were forgotten, for he loved to
have his nephew get off impromptus of that
sort.

Another time Heine was speaking of an
exchange broker who occasionally was a guest
at his uncle's table, had visited a university town
in his youth, was somewhat limited in wit, and
thought much of good eating, and he said : " Pity
that his learning only got as far as his throat."

Mathilde was glad when she got home again,
and declared to her husband that she did not
want to visit again the stiff, wearisome society at
his uncle's. Heine knew his stubborn little girl
and was in great embarrassment, because the

good will of his uncle was very important to him; he answered there was only one way out of it, namely, for her to return to Paris without him. As Mathilde insisted on her resolve, her husband was compelled to send her to her early boarding school in care of Mme. Darte at Paris, under the pretense that her mother was ill; and after a fortnight's stay Mathilde took leave of us, bathed in tears.

Heine remained in Hamburg and finished his book "Deutschland, ein Wintermärchen," a humorous epic, in which his impressions of the sea voyage of the year before were depicted, and which appeared with the "New Poems" in September, while he was staying in Hamburg.* The severe satirical lashing of the situation of affairs, at that time impossible to endure, aroused in many persons anger and vexation, but the majority on the other hand were astonished at his clever indestructible humor.

The "Wintermärchen" proved such a pleasure to his uncle Salomon that he made his nephew a round present of money and promised him that

* For the long poem "Deutschland" see vol. ii. pp. 211-278. —Tr.

the annual income which he received should be
continued to his wife after his death.

Heine took his meals usually in my parent's
house and often stayed there in the evening for
a jolly gossip over a cup of tea. My sister Anna,*
his favorite, made tea for him and had to suffer
particularly from his teasing.

Almost always he inquired: "Is this a cup of
tea such as you would have made for yourself, or
is it camomile tea?" Weary of this reiterated
teasing, she handed her uncle one day a cup of
real camomile tea, which he put down from his
lips, shuddering, while he exclaimed: "Boo!
the bread and butter Miss has taken her revenge!"

Heine's favorite haunt was the pavilion on the
Alsterbasin whither he went almost every day
and remained gossiping with his friends Dr. Wille,
Julius Campe, Dr. Fuchs, Michelis, Dr. Carl
Toepfer, Professor Zimmermann and the painter
Kizero.

Sometimes I was allowed to accompany him,
and then he sat either monosyllabic, dreamily
gazing down on the crinkled waves of the Alster,

* Mrs. Anna (Embden) Italiener, born in London.

following with his eyes a swan as it sailed by, or
talkative, giving me excellent hints of what books
I ought to select for my reading.   He warned me
against the reading of newspapers, since less of it
sticks in one's memory than what one gains from
any ordinary book.   He had a high regard for
Jean Paul—and I must read his works slowly and
carefully, which would bear fruit for my whole
life!   Moreover, he could not recommend me
enough to make myself acquainted with the
works of Charles Dickens in the absence from
the German of the rarely occurring novel of
comedy.

   This delightful propinquity came to an end too
soon for all of us, for Heine's French publishers
asked urgently for his presence in Paris, and
after a tender farewell he returned at the beginning of October on the steamer by way of Amsterdam to Paris.

XLIX

AMSTERDAM, October 11, 1844.

DEAREST MOTHER:

Amsterdam, which we should have reached
this morning, was not reached till seven this

afternoon. Still, I have had a very pleasant journey and was not sick at all. This very night I travel to the Hague and in two or three days I shall be in Paris, whence I shall not write you at once, as the rest of the journey now is child's play. I hope that these few lines written in the greatest haste will get away this evening. In any event you must have set your mind at rest about me some time ago, since you could see yourself how fine and quiet the weather was.

I write these few lines on the bench at the railway station and with a seasick pen.

I embrace Lotta. Greetings to all.

Your faithful son,
H. HEINE.

L

PARIS, October 17, 1844.

MY DEAR, KIND MOTHER:

I trust you received the letter which I wrote you on my arrival in Amsterdam. The rest of my journey was also favored by good weather, and yesterday evening I arrived in Paris in the best health at the side of my dear wife. I found her lively and in good health, and she has con-

ducted herself like a model of obedience just as I
arranged.   We are both still as if stunned by the
joy of seeing each other again!   We look at each
other with big, round eyes, laugh, embrace, talk
about you all, laugh again, and the parrot screams
in between like mad.   How glad I am to see both
my birds again!   You see, dear mother, I am as
happy as a man well can be, seeing there is
nothing perfect in this world.   All I need now is
a sound head and the presence of my kind
mother and my kind Lotta.   In a few days I
shall miss you still more; now I am filled too
much with the delight of coming back.

Tell Lotta that she must write me soon (*Faubourg Poissonière, No. 46*).   I shall only write to
her later, since I have nothing yet to report to
her and she will hear of my happy arrival from
this letter.   I greet the whole cabal—the chicks,
the boy, and very special compliments are to be
paid in my name and my wife's to my brother-in-
law, to whom my wife sends the warmest thanks
for his courteous attentions.

Only write to me soon how Uncle Heine is; I
left you all in such good health that I take yours
for granted.

A great pile of work awaits me here this minute and despite my vile headache I must strain every nerve for the next few months.

I have bought my wife a marvelous splendid family register, just such an album * as she has been long desiring. She promises to write you soon. Meantime God keep you and you will live long.

I embrace you, dear mother. Did Jette have to look to see what the wind was very often on Wednesday night?

H. HEINE.

LI

PARIS, October 24, 1844.

DEAR, KIND MOTHER:

I see nothing and hear nothing of my chest and yet I need the books that are in it. I pray you write me at once when and how that box left. I am, God be praised, in good health; my wife is also well. Kisses to Lotta and the children. We talk of you here all the time. Lotta will soon write me, I hope.

Your faithful son,

H. HEINE.

* For lines in Mathilde's album see vol. iii. p. 97.

LII

PARIS, November 28, 1844.

DEAR, KIND MOTHER:

My eyes were in bad case again, but are better now and in order to spare them I write little. Otherwise my wife and I are in good health. We are happy and of good cheer. Your last letter is received. Uncle's sickness makes me sad beyond conception; do write everything at once and often. I have your letter; I do not know what poem it can be which you mention; if it relates to me send it to me under separate cover. I beg you to forward the inclosure to Lotta.

It is late and very dark and my pen is much blacker than my heart.

*   *   *   *   *

H. HEINE.

LIII

PARIS, November 28, 1844.

MY DEAR, KIND SISTER:

I thank you for your letter of the 18th. I ought to have written to you long ago and at length. But unhappily my eye trouble had so wretchedly increased that only with the greatest effort could I write at all and I had nothing of urgent importance to say. My eye, which was shut entirely for three weeks, is now open again, but is still very weak; the trouble, however, seems periodical, and I shall certainly be quite free from it from time to time. Otherwise I am in excellent condition, have a good appetite, am very quiet, and live pleasantly in my domestic shell. The squanderer is as ever a kind child; honest, gay, only now and then given to a few whimsies. We are always talking about you all. And I cannot tell you how much my wife admires you all, particularly mother, who is a woman splendidly kind. Kiss her well in my name and my wife's. Kisses to your children too, and the heartiest greetings to your husband.

What you write me concerning uncle [Salomon Heine] is very sad. You can imagine my sorrow. At any risk you must not leave me without news of his condition; I expect a weekly bulletin from you. I beg you not to neglect to let me know as often as possible the mournful or pleasant news of the family; it is beyond all conception important to me. I did not imagine this, and my heart is very heavy in consequence.

My eye trouble, which came upon me immediately I arrived, is to blame that I did not write a minute report to Max, as I intended. I wanted to explain everything to him in a necessarily cautious and clearly stated way—and so it happened that I wrote not at all. But it is now a case in which it is your duty to report to him quickly and firmly uncle's condition ; tell him the truth. If there is hope that he may not come too late to fulfill the duties of filial attachment, perhaps he will now hasten thither quicker than before. I pray you write to him at once and keep him also *au courant* as to the condition of a health so dear to us.

And now farewell. As soon as my eyes permit I shall write more. Besides, it is so dark to-day ! A disgusting, loathsome month ! I await with anxiety your next letter. Greetings to all.

Your true brother,

H. HEINE.

LIV

PARIS, December 23, 1844.

DEAR CHILD :

Inclosed a letter to mother, the contents of which is for you too ! I burden you in addition

with a commission for Uncle Henry. I had sent
him a bill of exchange for one thousand marks
drawn on Campe, with the request that he should
discount it. Now my kind Uncle Henry sent
me yesterday the sum of money, but called my
attention to the fact that Campe had not yet
accepted it, and though not declining to do so,
was waiting for an answer from me to his last
letter.

Since then a difference of opinion has risen between us, which, it is to be hoped, only has a mis-
understanding at bottom, and which I explained
away in my reply. But since on this occasion I
have told him [Campe] very forcibly the truth
of the situation, it is just possible that he may
not accept my draft. So I wish you would tell
Uncle Henry that I thank him very heartily for
his confidence, but that in the above circumstances I shall not allow the draft on Fould received from him to be paid out to me until
I have received news through you that my bill
of exchange has been accepted by Campe. If
this is not done, I shall send back to Uncle
Henry his draft. Tell mother nothing about
this. Shall look out for myself better in my

dealings with Campe, although hitherto I have
had no dispute with him.

My wife has received a Christmas present from
Uncle Heine.

*   *   *   *   *

H. HEINE.

On the twenty-third of December 1844 Salomon Heine died, and the news of his decease
threw the poet, with his nervous temperament,
into great excitement.

Salomon Heine, born 1767 in Hanover, came to
Hamburg without means, established himself as
an exchange broker after preparing himself for
mercantile pursuits, founded the at one time
world-famous banking house, and died a millionaire several times over. He was very generally
regretted owing to his many works of benev-
olence. His most prominent foundations are
the Hermann Heine Loan Institute in memory
of his son who died in Rome as early as 1830,
and the Hamburg Hospital for Israelites * in
memory of his wife, Betty Goldschmidt.

* See vol. ii. p. 106, for Heine's bitter verses suggested by this
hospital.—TR.

LV

PARIS, December 29, 1844.

DEAR, KIND SISTER:

Late yesterday evening I received your letter. You can easily imagine what a frightful night I have passed. My brain is trembling in my head. I am not able yet to put two thoughts together. Although I was prepared for the catastrophe, still it has shaken me so deeply as no event has moved me since the death of my father. I am amazed that you can write me at once under all your sorrow.

You weep; but so far I have not been able to shed a tear. You women have this advantage, you can weep easier than men. My wife is crying too; thrice this night has she come to my room. You are right in saying that time alone can console us under this affliction. How must not that good woman Therese * suffer!

* Therese, the youngest of Salomon Heine's daughters (died 1880) was as little an unhappy youthful love of Heinrich Heine as her older sister, who died before her—Mrs. Amalie Friedländer. Certain quotations from his poems may very possibly have reference to Amalie, who was beautiful and clever according to every account and was highly esteemed by the poet. [But see letter cix. for the endeavors of the family to keep Therese from Heine's sick-bed in 1853.—TR.]

And Carl, the poor boy, how much must he have undergone! I shall not write to the poor children until I am controlled and quiet. My God, what a sorrow!

And dear Uncle Henry, how this must fall upon him! Tell him everything that is affectionate. My head will not yet permit me to send condolences. The pen shakes in my hand. Moreover, my eyes are in the most frightful condition again. Oh, if I could only weep.

It was only yesterday that I wrote to him, although I had a premonition of disaster. Let me have all the details of his last moments. This man has played a great rôle in the history of my life and shall be depicted in a way none shall forget. What a heart! What a brain! Concerning his last arrangements I have long been without anxiety; he himself has told me enough about it or clearly given me to understand. I would give my last shilling if I could only have kept him alive five years, or even only three years more; yes, I would have given the half of my remaining years of life for that satisfaction. And how charmingly he treated my poor mother!

He said many harsh things to me; in his excitement he even gave me a blow with his cane—my God, how gladly would I not take my blows again! If I could only cry!

I am awaiting with anxiety the woeful letter from mother, who, I know her so well, will not be quieted soon and is now tearing open all the old wounds. Only do you write me at once how Carl is getting on; and about Therese too, who along with all her firmness is still a tender creature and has already borne much. Her father was all in all to her and she is so like him in her whole nature. Farewell, and write me at once. I have nothing to say to you to-day; am nothing but a sloppy dishrag to-day.

I have always been steeled against this occurrence and long ago repeated to myself everything that can comfort us—and yet the disaster falls upon me as if it were quite unexpected, quite impossible. Yes, I know it is quite true, that I have lost him, but I cannot believe it yet.

Greetings to your husband. Kiss the two dear children. Would like to say something gay to them, but to-day all fun is out of me.

Your brother,

H. HEINE.

The sudden news of the death of his uncle Salomon, and the fact that there was no allusion in the will, as his uncle had promised, to a continuation of the annual allowance, had a crushing effect on Heine's health. His only son Carl, who was the chief heir *more Judaico*, declined to continue the payment and had also ordered withheld the small legacy of eight thousand marks which in accordance with the terms of the will went legally to Heine, because the latter threatened to obtain his rights by way of the law.

When they besought Heine not to push the matter to the last point, but to compose the difference of opinion with his cousin by attempts at a compromise, he wrote to Hamburg : " I know Carl Heine better than you; he is as stubborn as he is secretive. One cannot get at him on the line of ambition, for in this respect he is the opposite of his father, who flattered public opinion like a courtier, while it is entirely indifferent to my cousin what the people say. He has but three passions—women, cigars and quiet. I cannot take from him the two former—but his quiet [I can] and it is just a lawsuit that serves my purpose."

Both were hot-headed, and it was not till two years later, after many troublesome efforts of his sister Charlotte and various friends, that an understanding with Carl Heine took place. It was agreed to pay an allowance of four thousand francs *prænumerando*, one-half of which was to continue for his widow after the death of the poet.

Carl Heine was a man of violent temper but good heart, and the poet's complaints of his knavery were unjust. When Heine's sickness got worse and his nursing cost great outlays, Carl Heine raised the pension voluntarily to eight thousand francs, and Mathilde received as widow not the half allowance stipulated, but every year till the end of her life the sum of five thousand francs—probably in remembrance of the fact that when in 1832 the cholera was raging at Paris and Carl Heine had fallen sick of it and was in peril of his life, his health was restored to him only through the self-sacrificing nursing of his cousin Heinrich.

Heine's sickness was very badly heightened by the continuous state of excitement, but a water cure saved him; and in hopes of entire con-

valescence, he had moved into a country house at
the order of his physician.

LVI

PARIS, June 24, 1845.

MY DEAR, KIND MOTHER:

Since about a fortnight I have been living at
Montmorency and get rarely into the city.
Yesterday evening I came in and heard that a
German letter had been forwarded to me at
Montmorency, and I suppose that the letter is
from you; I shall get it to-morrow, and if it be
necessary shall answer it later; if not, then content yourself with the news that we are in good
health. I have a little country house in Montmorency with a pretty garden—a veritable
paradise *en miniature*. My wife conducts herself
most affectionately and amuses herself with the
flowers. My parrot screeches rather too much.

My left eye is still closed. I am using sulphur
baths, which are excellent for me. I can scarcely
write at all with the pen I am using to-day; but
I must not leave you too long without a letter.
I hope that you and Lotta are in good health.

You must walk a great deal. We talk of you constantly, and you have no conception how my wife loves you. Do write me soon how things are with you. I do very little—write nothing!

Farewell and keep in affection

Your faithful son,

H. HEINE.

LVII

PARIS, October 31, 1845.

DEAR, PRECIOUS MOTHER:

Again you are getting very lazy about writing. Your silence makes me still more anxious in a season when the weather itself puts one in bad humor. I hope that you and Lotta are in good case. Things go on here as usual. Nothing noteworthy has happened since I wrote. My wife is well; indeed, I hope that her illness has entirely forsaken her. We dwell here quiet, peaceful and well, are much at home and recall you in our long winter-evening talks.

'Tis to be hoped that this year will slink off quietly without any new blows; it has been a vile year.

Greet my dear sister heartily; I have nothing

to remark to her, otherwise I should write to her. But she must not leave me without a letter.

My wife asks to be remembered. At the moment she is occupied in hemming my bedclothes; linen is her hobby.

Your faithful son,

H. HEINE.

LVIII

PARIS, April 23, 1846.

DEAREST, KIND MOTHER:

I duly received your last letter a fortnight ago and saw that you were well. Not a little am I astonished that your companion Jette is about to don the married woman's cap and will leave you. I shall be in much worry until I hear from you that she has been satisfactorily replaced. I hope that nothing else disagreeable has happened, and that Lotta is well. Things go on with me as usual; my trouble draws downward to the lower parts of the face, toward my mouth. But I am fresh and sound at heart; I intend this year to make a trip to the baths and so do something really serious toward my complete restoration.

I hardly work at all; that is certainly the best I can do. Probably I shall leave about the middle of next month.

My wife is in pretty good condition; only for the last two days the little birds that grunt have been sounding their pipes a bit. I have moved and am now living a little more comfortably on the same street. My address is *41 Faubourg Pois-sonière.* Write me soon, so that the letter may catch me in Paris.

My wife asks to be tenderly remembered.

Your faithful son,
H. HEINE.

LIX

PARIS, December 26, 1846.

DEAR, KIND MOTHER:

We are at the close of the old year, which has done us as little good as its forerunner. May the new year conduct itself better! In any event, I congratulate you and our dear Lotta on this change of season. My wife also asks me to tell and wish you everything that is most kind. We embrace you with the most profound tenderness. My wife is now quite well in health and things

get on much better with me. I drink and eat
with a good appetite and have cleared out all
the physicians. We live quietly and in the best
unity. Talk of you all the time.

Inclosed a letter which I beg you to send to
Campe.

*　　*　　*　　*　　*

H. HEINE.

LX

PARIS, February 28, 1847.

DEAR, KIND GLORY OF A MOTHER!

Your and Lotta's last letters, in which is the
reply to my questions for Campe, has been
duly received, and I thank you heartily, dear
Lotta, for its prompt furtherance. I have now
found a means to secure an immediate answer
from you both—namely, by giving you a commission. I hope you are both in the best of
health. A savage cold has set in here which is
not exactly favorable to me. Still, I keep pretty
well, my condition improves *peu à peu*, and I look
forward to an agreeable spring and summer.
Only my poor eyes are suffering very much, or
rather the convulsive paralysis drags my eyelids

down more and more, so that I am seeing very badly ; the eyes themselves are sound.

I am now on entirely good terms with Carl Heine ; indeed, I am even satisfied with him ! Not only is he to pay me the pension which I received from his father down to the end of my life, but he has besides imparted to me the solemn promise that after my death (God preserve me !) the half of the sum, namely two thousand four hundred francs, shall go to my wife for life if she survives me. I am more pleased with that than if he had made me a present of a large sum of money. It is a great question, 'tis true, if she do survive me ; but she is so spoiled and inexperienced that I cannot sufficiently care for her. If she had more sense, I would have occupied myself less with her future ; and here again you see how foolishness is a happy gift from God, for other persons must look out for the foolish. My business looks well in other respects. I do not mean the stock exchange, from which I have withdrawn with a black eye !

We are always talking here about you and dear Lotta and the children. May God preserve you !

Fine compliments to my brother-in-law
Moritz, particularly from my wife, whose head
has been quite turned by him. Carl was surprised to hear with what enthusiasm my wife
talked of Moritz; he also spoke of him in
praise.

And now farewell, and keep me in affection.

H. HEINE.

LXI

PARIS, March 27, 1847.

DEAR, KIND MOTHER:

For some days the most marvelous fine weather
has favored us here, but it is still too sultry to be
healthy; the whole world is more or less out of
kilter, and for my part I am still suffering with
my eyes. You cannot conceive how unpleasant
it is not to be allowed to read, and also not to go
to the theater because of the frightful gas lights;
here I sit every evening *en tête-à-tête* with my
wife, who has to take the place of all other
amusements. I have hired a wondrous fine
country place at Montmorency; it costs likewise
a wondrous fine sum, one thousand francs for the
season, and in May I shall move out there and

give myself up to the most complete, nerve strengthening quiet.

And how are things with you? Only write me lots. Lotta also is thanked for every line she writes me.

I have published " Atta Troll " in French, and it is an incredible success.

Farewell; I must now go out for a walk in this beautiful weather.

Your loving, faithful,

H. HEINE.

Heine wrote in the preface to the French issue: " 'Atta Troll' was written in 1841 at a time when the so-called political poesy bloomed. The opposition sold out its junk shop and turned to poesy. The Muses received the most strict orders no longer to loaf about in a lazy and frivolous way, but to enter into the service of the fatherland, as who should say the market women of liberty, or the laundresses of the truly Christian and Germanic nation! By the eternal gods! at that time it was necessary to stand up for the inalienable rights of the intellect, especially in poetry. As this stand was the grand purpose of

my life, I have naturally least of all lost sight
of it in the present poem, and the prosody,
as well as the contents thereof, was a protest
against the *plebiscita* held by the journalistic
tribunes of the day.

"And in fact, the very first fragments of 'Atta
Troll' which were printed roused the spleen of
my character-heroes, of my Romans, who accused
me not merely of a literary but of a social
reaction; yea verily, of scorn for the most holy
ideas concerning mankind! With respect to the
æsthetic value of my poem, I gladly gave that
up, and wrote it for my own joy and delectation
in the fantastic dream-method of that romantic
school in which I have passed the pleasantest of
my youthful years. In this respect, perhaps, my
poem is damnable. But thou liest, Brutus; thou
liest, Cassius; and, Asinius, thou liest likewise,
when ye maintain that my jesting is aimed at
those ideas which are a valuable gain made by
mankind, for the which I myself have battled and
suffered so much! No, just because those ideas
are always floating before the poet with the most
beautiful distinctness, just so much the more
irresistible is the desire to laugh which seizes

him when he perceives how rudely, lumpishly and lubberly these very ideas have been conceived by the narrow minds of his contemporaries. Then he jokes, as it were, across their temporal bearskins. There are mirrors which are ground at such a slant that an Apollo himself must be reflected in them as a caricature and compel our laughter. But then we laugh at the distorted picture, not the god."

LXII

PARIS, April 19, 1847.

DEAREST, KIND MOTHER:

I have received your letter of the 13th, and see with delight that you are in good health and moreover that Madame Gustav has calved. I send him congratulations through you. So far he has been able to engender girls only; that is nothing; I, had I wished, might have been at present the father of nine daughters just as well as Apollo who engendered the nine Muses. I hear nothing but good of Gustav from Vienna; he is getting on splendidly, it seems. Formerly I heard with great bewilderment that he was liv-

ing in a very economical way ('tis true I thought
of the commissioner). Greet him heartily for
me ; I often think of him, and it was only yester-
night that I recollected how once as a little boy
he assured us that he loved his mother more
than his cat; nay, that he loved her more than
six cats !

My dear Lotta I embrace fraternally as well as
the children.   I am gay and well, but rail against
the world ; and if by chance you hear that I am
on a diet of grass, be assured that I am only
taking a bite at a good cooky !

Unhappily, nothing is changed as regards my
eyes; it is the cramp also that affects the mouth ;
probably it will vanish under the nerve-sooth-
ing air and quiet of the country.   I shall permit
no doctors near me any more.   I notice that all
the people who have died this winter have had a
physician !

At the present moment, while I am preparing
to move into the country, I am employed with
the arrangement of my papers. This time I am
going through all my letters again and burning
all in which the slightest thing occurs which
might be taken up, especially in family matters.

Unhappily I have been forced to give to the flames a part of the letters from you and almost all of those from Lotta; a thing that hurt me grievously, since I love you both more than—six cats!

As you know, I have published "Atta Troll' in French and am delighted by the extraordinary applause it has found. Greet Max for me when you write, and I pray you send me again his address at St. Petersburg; I mislaid it and want to spare myself the trouble of looking it up.

Just now my wife came in (she lives six rooms away from my workroom) and without my telling it noticed that I was writing to you two and asked to be remembered with many kisses and tender words.

This cat also I love more than six other cats. She asks particularly to be remembered to my brother-in-law and on the same occasion I also add a few greetings for Moritz. Dear Lotta, you have no conception how very favorably my wife was impressed by your husband. She also sends her greetings to Ludwig, worshipful my nephew.

Your faithful

H. HEINE.

LXIII

PARIS, May 8, 1847.

DEAREST, KIND MOTHER :

I thought to have an occasion to send something to Hamburg and so I arranged for the purpose a little chest in which were two silk dresses,
a black gown for you, and a violet-hued, bright-
colored robe for my dear Lotta. But as the occasion did not turn up I put the little chest into the
straight postal road in order that perchance you
may get it by way of Havre.

Although I gave orders to prepay it at Havre
(one cannot prepay through to Hamburg from
here) I do not know whether that has been done,
and perhaps, dear mother, you have been compelled to pay a heavy expressage. Tell me if
this has been the case. I and my wife looked up
the gowns ourselves and my wife enjoyed herself
like a child doing it ; and she hopes that Lotta will
agree with her taste. It is understood that in no
case have I reckoned on *your* agreement, and I
shall be satisfied if you do not scold me about it !

We greet and kiss you both.

True and loving !

H. HEINE.

LXIV

MONTMORENCY, June 7, 1847.

DEAREST, KIND MOTHER:

Your and Lotta's kind letter, in which the reception of my small chest is announced, was received here duly at the proper time, since for the last three weeks I have been here in my country place so marvelous fine, where I enjoy the pleasantest and most comfortable existence.

A big garden, almost a park, where are tall trees in which the "nightingoles," as old Nathan David of Copenhagen used to say, sing in most delightful fashion. And meantime I do nothing and take care of my health.

You see that you need be under no anxiety on my account. My wife is as jolly withal as a monkey, brightens the hours in which I am low-spirited, and indeed conducts herself excellently. Were it not for my eye trouble, which compels me to deny myself all reading, I would lack for nothing—unless it be my mother and sister; but we talk constantly about you with the most profound affection.

At this moment a ballet by me is being rehearsed in London at Her Majesty's Theater. As it has already been paid for by the manager (and with an enormously big sum) I shall await the result quite without disquiet; if it be a brilliant success, as expected, there springs up for me in England a new source of pecuniary help, the like of which till now I have never found in Germany, and also not in France. I kiss heartily my dear Lotta and her children.

My wife, that charming squanderer, asks to be remembered heartily to you all, and particularly to my brother-in-law. My parrot screams at this moment as if he also wished to have his compliments forwarded to Hamburg.

Your

H. HEINE.

LXV

MONTMORENCY, June 22, 1847.

DEAREST, KIND, HONEST MOTHER:

I know not why, but for several days the thought has been torturing me that you might be out of sorts, and I will confess that I would I had a letter from you ere this ! So don't let me wait long for news of you. Since I have suffered so much from my eyes, I write with nicely whittled feather nibs, which the devil fly away with! for among the score there is scarcely one that is good.

My kind cat asks to be heartily remembered. She is happy to have a country place with so big and beautiful a garden where she can occupy herself from early morn to late evening with watering, gathering fruit, with planting and pruning ; she wears a big brown straw hat and is the most innocent delightfulness in person.

I kiss my dear Lotta—but write, write, write

Your

H. HEINE.

LXVI

MONTMORENCY, July 27, 1847.

DEAREST, KIND MOTHER :

If I write you little at present, that comes from the fact that I have really nothing profitable to impart ; besides, since living in the country I have become so lazy that I have a regular loathing for ink and pen. I am on the whole well, but my eye trouble is stubborn. I must read almost not at all ; writing likewise is not particularly wholesome for me.

This winter in Paris I shall procure a reader, who can also serve as a secretary. If therefore you get a letter from me some day which is not in my handwriting, do not be scared; I give you warning six months in advance. I hope that in your last letter (which you addressed directly hither) you told the truth and are really in good health. You have no idea how I worry very often when I think of you. I go to Paris rarely, and live here, quiet and peaceful, in my country state; I care for myself with conscientiousness.

A disgracefully bad rain storm has been going for two days, and the little grunty birds are piping with my wife. She loves you and Lotta unspeakably and we talk of you constantly. Her conduct is excellent barring a slight indulgence in moods and the worst of prodigality. All the same, since I have no children she only squanders her own money after all, since I shall leave her less at my death than I would had she been economical!

I greet my dear Lotta and the children heartily. Ah, if to-day I only had a little barley soup such as one can eat at Lotta's house, or an *Auflauf* such as Anna loves to eat! Farewell, and write directly to me here at Montmorency at the given address.

Rain is falling from the sky as if from buckets.

Your faithful

H. HEINE.

LXVII

MONTMORENCY, September 21, 1847.

DEAREST, KIND MOTHER:

Your nice letter of the third of the month was received all right and I perceive therefrom with pleasure that you are well. I am getting from Germany various letters of good wishes in which I am congratulated on the complete restoration of my health; what this refers to I know not, since it is months that I have not read a line.

I notify you to-day that in three days I shall leave Montmorency again owing to the approaching wet and frosty season. For the time being I shall move again into my old dwelling (*Faubourg Poissonière No. 41*), whither you are to address all your letters. But about the beginning of October I shall have a new house and will notify you just as soon as I have moved in without mishap. What a bang and bounce and dingdong in order to make the shreds of life a little bearable! My wife asks to be remembered; she is very busy. She and the parrot scold all the day long—but I have need of both. My eyes are still suffering and I cannot read. Do write me often and much, but I warn you beforehand—can't write much!

I greet heartily my dear, darling Lotta, and send kisses by her to all her children. My wife has solemnly bound me to send extra greetings to my nephew beside those for the entire gossipred. For my brother-in-law Moritz likewise the friendliest greetings!

Your faithful

H. HEINE.

LXVIII

PARIS, October 28, 1847.

DEAR, KIND MOTHER:

I am living now 21 *Rue de la Victoire*—that's the main thing I have to report to you to-day.

Just think—the twenty-first of last month I left Montmorency and moved into my old lodgings, and a fortnight ago I had to leave them again and move into new quarters. So I have been moving twice! What a burden for my poor wife! In the midst of this bother my maid-servant left, and for ten days my wife had to perform her work! So now she is as if beaten to pieces and in consequence I am very woeful. Otherwise, however, things go nicely with us. My eyes are always in a suffering state. Your letter was duly received with the inclosure from Christiani. His eye troubles are from a very different source. This winter I shall try something better.

Farewell! Dear Lotta, I kiss you, and you, dear mother, I kiss twice!

Your obedient son,
H. HEINE.

LXIX

PARIS, November 6, 1847.

DEAREST, KIND MOTHER:

Your and Lotta's letter of the eleventh of the month was duly received, and with great sorrow I find that you have been ill and perhaps are not yet restored to health. The frightfulest thing in being separated is that at a distance one imagines the sufferings of one's dear ones as much greater than if they were near, where the mere sight of them acts as a comfort. I pray you, dearest mother, to write me at once, or let some-one write at once, how things are with you—the strictest truth—for I can stand everything except uncertainty. I do not understand how my delay in writing could have disquieted you; long ago I prepared you for the fact that in this season all possible bangs and bounces fall on my shoulders.

My new dwelling is finer but smaller than the other; so far I am satisfied with it (*Rue de la Victoire*, 21, *Ter*).

To you, dear Lotta, heartiest thanks for the last two letters; only do write me a great deal, particularly in regard to the family, because here I learn nothing. Your project to visit me here de-lights me; my wife also is beside herself with joy.

But to-day I shall write you little in this matter, since I suffer to-day more than com-monly with my eyes. But I will write you next time at length concerning the carrying out of your plan. Write me, dear Lotta, your present address, since I shall probably have to give some-one a letter of introduction to you and never know the address.

Your husband as well as the children and my Sir Nephew are to be greeted for me. My wife sends kisses *in blanco*. Farewell, and keep me in affection.

Oh, if only my old Mausel* were in good health once more!

H. HEINE.

LXX

PARIS, December 4, 1847.

DEAR, KIND MOTHER :

I perceive with pleasure from your last letter that you are on the way to betterment, and I hope that you have told the truth. With regard to my health, I am always suffering with my eyes, but in other respects I am in better case than usual. Indeed for the last two years I have not felt so young and well from my heart as I have the last fortnight ; that comes from the draft of herbs which I am now drinking as a cure and which, according to the assurances of my physician, will radically restore me ; so that I look forward to a good winter. As soon as my cure is finished I will tell you more about it. I have a pen with which I am not able to write and, moreover, cannot cut myself another, since un-

* Affectionate name for his mother. —TR.

fortunately my house is not a very light one—
the latter is in general not up to my desires, since,
particularly to-day, I am always within sound of
knocking.

Unless I am mistaken your birthday ought to
fall somewhere hereabout and I send you my
wishes for good luck with the heartiest love. As
I do not know that I shall write to you before
New Year's, I am congratulating you twice over
on this occasion. What shall I present to you on
Christmas ? A candelabrum of crystal for your
drawing room, or a Turkish carpet ? I saw one
yesterday that only cost eight thousand francs.
My wife has already bought my Christmas present
(with the money she has laid by), namely, a magnificent night-chair, which is really so magnificent that
the goddess Hammonia * would not be ashamed
of it. I would not swap it against the throne of
the King of Prussia, and sit upon it quiet and safe.

*   *   *   *   *

I kiss my dear Lotta as well as the children.
Write to me soon, my good, dear old Mausel !

Your faithful

H. HEINE.

* Tutelary goddess and patron saint of Hamburg.—TR.

LXXI

PARIS, December 29, 1847.

DEAREST, KIND MOTHER:

I am always writing to you under the most vexatious external hindrances, for in my house the knocking never ceases and the chimneys smoke. So I shall move as soon as I can find a new house.

My cure begins to tell fairly, but my eyes are still always suffering; wherefore I am able to write but little. Wiesbaden can do me no good. Christiani's recovery there is a special matter of its own. Christiani gambled at Wiesbaden, and when he had gambled away all his money there —suddenly his eyes were opened!!

My kind wife asks to congratulate you and my dear sister on the new year. We wish happiness and blessing to you!

Do write to me soon; I am very sorrowful when I remain a few weeks without a letter from you two! The old departing year was a vile one! The devil take it!

Write, write! Soon, soon!

Your obedient son,

H. HEINE.

LXXII

PARIS, January 19, 1848.

DEAR, KIND MOTHER :

Your last letter containing good wishes for the new year was duly received and I hope that the report of your good health is the truth. So far as I am concerned I find myself better than usual, very much better, and though the cure does not work so quickly on my eyes as I could wish, yet it has already relieved me of several troubles, such as pains in the lower stomach, headache, and the like. In a few days I must move out again ; my infamous landlord has quartered his horses under my sleeping chamber contrary to right and compact, and these stamp the whole night through and rob me of my sleep. I pass the whole day outside the house on account of the banging. I write in a hurry before going out, and it is still dark at nine o'clock. My poor wife was very sick yesterday. What I must bear with !

Just now my wife had me called ; she has passed a good night and I hope she will soon feel her wings again. Yesterday she had an attack of the nerves, and she bit through with her teeth in a cramp-like way the glass of water which was held to her lips for refreshment ; they had to tear the bits of glass out of her mouth ! Imagine my terror ! I trust that no splinter has been left. Nothing but scares and unpleasantnesses ! What I bear with ! Often human life hangs on a single thread !

In the English papers they have got me dead again and regret very much my early demise. In the German papers I am at least three-quarters dead. I am used to this sort of thing now.

I kiss you, dear Lotta, and beg that you will write me a good deal, especially about dear mother. As soon as I move into the new house I will notify you of the new address.

Your faithful

H. HEINE.

LXXIII

PARIS, January 27, 1848.

DEAR, KIND MOTHER :

I only want to tell you hurriedly that in a few days I shall move into my new house and that my address is *Rue de Berlin, No. 9, à Paris.*

Write me therefore soon. My dear wife is quite restored again and scolds as much as ever. We live very peacefully for the most part, but she worries me in small matters. Particularly I have to support a great deal from her love of cleanliness, and then she reminds me not seldom of squinting Nan, who drove me to madness with her *schrubben*.

I expect a big letter from you, dear Lotta, and meantime I kiss you and the chicks. I still find that I am well; but my original cure has been neutralized by the scare and the constant noise in the house.

I love you unspeakably, my dear, good mother!

H. Heine.

Heine concealed from his old mother the true facts of his health, excusing the illegible writing by bad pens, and described his severe sufferings as a temporary indisposition. The miraculous draft of Dr. Sichel did not have the promised action, and just as little did the water cure of Dr. Wertheim.

Heine now took for his physician Dr. Gruby, a Hungarian, and at his suggestion entered the

private hospital of his friend Faultrier. Frightful cramps, beginning at the head and raging
through the whole body down to the feet, made
large doses of morphia necessary in order to obtain a merely passing alleviation. In the midst of
these violent sufferings the February Revolution
suddenly broke out. Heine, no less surprised
than all the rest of the world, said concerning the
fall of Louis Philippe : " Luck in war is rare with
old people ; Louis Philippe skedaddled in the
first confusion of the battle, and so we found ourselves in the Republic, without knowing what
had happened to us."

Heine stayed at his friend Faultrier's place
till the end of March, and then in May, somewhat
strengthened, moved into a country place at
Passy.

LXXIV

PARIS, March 30, 1848.

DEAREST, KIND MOTHER :

Just because it is so stormy in the world and
things are particularly turbulent here, I can write
you but little. The row has reduced me very
much, physically and morally. I am discouraged

as never before. Want to live quite still now
and bother my head about nothing more. Right
in the midst of the crisis of my cure the hubbub
began and I have paid not only in money but
also in health. Should matters turn still more
gloomy, as I fear, I shall depart with my wife, or
else alone. Am very grumpy. In Germany too
it must not be very agreeable, and thither I have
no great longing either. My wife is well. We
live quietly and apart from the world. In no
circumstances shall I put myself forward. Notwithstanding, I am much slandered by the Germans here. They are screaming because I
accepted money from the fallen government,
since my name is on the list of pensioners.

The weather is marvelous fine and I walk a
great deal. My household goes along in its quiet
jog trot. My wife conducts herself well. If she
did not conduct herself well, I would give her
her freedom now, as all the kings now give their
peoples liberty ; then she would soon see what is
the upshot of freedom ! *

You have no idea what *misère* prevails here now.

* For a charming little poem on his wife, see vol. iii. p. 267.—
Tr.

The whole world is becoming free and bankrupt. Farewell !

Do write me a great deal, dear mother. And you too, dear Lotta. But don't reckon on news from me; I take up the pen only too unwillingly. Am afraid of writing. In order to make my address still more distinct, write down: To H. Heine *chez Mr. Faultrier,* 84 *Rue de Lourcine, à Paris.* I have all my letters addressed in that way now, because I do not trust my house porter. Did the family lose much money? Do write me a good deal, dear Lotta, and kiss the children. My wife sends hearty greetings.

H. HEINE.

The February Revolution at first enlivened Heine with a new enthusiasm of youth, and he moaned : "What a piece of bad luck to witness such a revolution in my condition! I ought to have been dead, or else well." His report of the three great February days to the *Allgemeine Zeitung* began: "My head was as if stunned— endless drumming, shooting and Marseillaise ! The last, that unceasing song, almost split my brain, and alas! a mob of thoughts most perilous to governments, which I had held imprisoned there for years, broke their way again to light!"

But from his letters to his mother alone one can see that the revolutionary chaos which aggravated the poet's nervous trouble soon occasioned a reaction from his happy feelings; and this disgust increased when the *Allgemeine Zeitung*, referring to an article in the French journal *Revue Rétrospective*, cast a bad light on Heine's view of the situation.

Publications from the archives of the last government under the ministry of Guizot showed that several persons enjoyed pensions from the fallen government, and among them Heine too, and from the same budget which afforded support to Gustavson the ex-King of Sweden, Prince Godoy, the famous historian Augustin Thierry and many political refugees and artists; among Germans to Dr. Weil, editor of the *Stuttgarter Zeitung*, Schmieder, counsel to the legation and to Baron von Klindworth.

Quite lately the accusations made at that time have been repeated; they were charges which Heine met by a public statement in the *Allgemeine Zeitung* of Augsburg. As this is

not known to everyone it is given at full length
here.

EXPLANATION.

"For some little time the *Revue Retrospective*
has been amusing itself with the publication of
papers from the archives of the late government
and among others it has also made public the
accounts of the Ministry of Foreign Affairs
during the leadership of Guizot.

"The fact that the name of the undersigned
was given together with a certain sum of money
opened a wide field for suspicions of the most
hateful kind, and a malicious putting of two
and two together, for which there was no warrant
in the *Revue Rétrospective.* This has served a
correspondent of the *Allgemeine Zeitung* the
foolish purpose of an accusation which, without
beating about the bush, points to this: that
Guizot's Ministry had bought my pen for certain sums of money in order to defend the
measures of its government. The editors of the
Allgemeine Zeitung accompany this correspondence with a note in which the opinion is
uttered that I may have received that subsidy

not so much for what I wrote as for that which
I did not write.

"The editors of the *Allgemeine Zeitung*, who
for twenty years have had abundant occasion to
remark (not so much through that part of my
writings which they printed as, far more, by that
which they declined to print) that I am not a
servile writer who would allow his silence to be
bought—the said editors at any rate might have
spared me that *levis nota*. I do not offer these
lines in answer to the article of the correspondent, but to the editorial note, and will explain as
distinctly as possible my relations to the ministry of Guizot. Higher interests determine me to
take this step—not the little matter of my personal safety, not even the question of honor.
My honor is not in the keeping of the next best
newspaper correspondent; nor is the next best
daily journal the court for it: I can be judged
only before the assizes of the history of literature.
Besides, I cannot admit that generosity shall be
interpreted as fear and reviled as such.

"No; the support which I received from the
Guizot administration was no tribute; it was
merely a support; it was—I am calling things

by their right names—the splendid alms which
the French people have distributed to so many
thousands of strangers who through their zeal for
the cause of Revolution have been more or less
gloriously compromised in their own homes and
have sought an asylum at the hospitable hearth of
France. I accepted such support in money soon
after the time when those regrettable decrees
of the Bundestag appeared which sought to ruin
me financially as the leader of the band of so-
called Young Germany, decrees which laid under
ban not only my existing writings but in
advance all other writings which might come
later from my pen, aiming by this means to
rob me without right or verdict of the means of
existence. The reason that the payment of the
assistance in money was assigned to the budget
of the Ministry of Foreign Affairs and moreover
to the fund for pensions, which is not submitted to public examination, lay chiefly in this,
that at the moment the other budgets were too
heavily laden. Perhaps, too, the French Government did not wish to support publicly a man
who was always a thorn in the side of the German legations and whose banishment had been

demanded on many occasions. It is widely
known how urgently my most royal and Prussian
friends enlightened the French Government
with such claims. But Mr. Guizot refused stiff-
neckedly my banishment and paid me my pension every month, regularly, without an omission.
Never did he demand from me the slightest
service in return ! When I waited upon him
soon after he had taken the portfolio of Foreign
Affairs, and thanked him for having notified me
of the continuance of my pension notwithstanding
the Radical complexion of my views, he answered
me with a kindly melancholy : ' I am not a
person to refuse a German poet who lives in
exile a bit of bread.' These words were said
to me by Mr. Guizot in November 1840, and this
was the first and last time in my life that I had
the honor of speaking to him.

   " I have given the editors of the *Revue Rétrospective* the proofs which establish the truth of the
above explanations, and they can now, as French
loyauté demands, speak their minds from the authentic sources which are open to them as to the
meaning and origin of the pension in question.

" H. HEINE.

   " PARIS, May 15, 1848."

LXXV

PASSY, May 27, 1848.

DEAR, KIND MOTHER:

For the last three days I have been living at Passy in a house with garden ; the place is distant half an hour from Paris. I do not know whether I have hit it off rightly with this dwelling, and whether new disturbances will not embitter my life here. Up to the present, bad luck has always followed me with every change of dwelling. For the moment, things go fairly with me. I write you these lines in the open air, under a green arbor, where the sunshine plays on my paper—a very pretty effect, but it bothers me a good deal in writing. My eye trouble, and in general the paralysis of the muscles of my face, are momentarily in their most insufferable bloom, and for that reason my poor wife has to bear a good deal from my grumpiness. Yet just now we have breakfasted together at the same table on which I am now writing, and we have been enjoying greatly our domestic quiet—as well as fine asparagus and strawberries!

How are things with you ? How does dear

Lotta get on these terrible times? Are you sure you have enough sugar so that the strawberries can lie comfortably and be warmly tucked in?

This year is no saccharine one, and the whole world finds a bitter taste in the mouth.

I take no bother for anything, and my disease itself perhaps protects me at this moment from fatal dangers to which I might have been exposed had I been able to plunge into the daily battles—crazed and well!

I have a letter from Gustav and his wife; he asserts that he is a happy father of a family and in the enjoyment of the greatest domestic bliss.

*   *   *   *   *

My address now is 64 *grande Rue à Passy, près de Paris.* Write me soon and much. I end here and kiss you both, as well as the children.

At this moment the rays of sunlight dazzle me too much. The parrot is screaming and my wife sends regards.

Your faithful

H. HEINE.

LXXVI

PASSY, June 10, 1848.

DEAREST SISTER:

My wife desires that I should not keep you any longer in a state of too great deception regarding the facts of my health, a deception which was necessary owing to mother; so that if I die you should not be too much horrified. But that extreme, dear child, will not occur so very soon, it is to be hoped, and I can still drag myself through life for a dozen years more just as I am—God's pity! Have been so lame for a fortnight that I have to be carried like a child; my legs are like cotton. My eyes horribly bad. Internally, however, I am well, and brain and stomach are sound. Am well cared for and have lack of nothing to meet the great expenses of sickness; . . .

My wife conducts herself admirably, and we live very pleasantly. If I die in this condition, my end will be still far better than that of a thousand other people. Now you know where you stand.

Gladly would I have visited you this summer;

perhaps I shall see you the coming spring, or
perhaps you will be coming hither next year.
This year I am at bottom glad not to be able to
see you here, on account of the rumblings of the
world's revolution which you must have to bear
quite as much as we do here. Yes, we live in a
wretched period, and I want to enjoy a sight of
you again while I am gay and well—not just for
a few sickly moments. But shall I ever be
better? God, who guides all things for the best,
alone knows that. Write me often and at length
how everything is in the family. Now as earlier
let us conceal my sickness from mother.

*   *   *   *   *

> Shadowy kisses, shadowy passion,
> Lives of shadow passing strange!
> Deem you, sister, things their fashion
> True shall keep with never a change?
>
> Things we kept in warm affection,
> Like to dream shapes off they sweep.
> Hearts forget each predilection
> And our eyelids close in sleep.*

H. HEINE.

Quiet was necessary in Heine's nervous condition, for the noisy life of Paris, where crowds

* See vol. ii. p. 32. The words are the same except that *Schwes-*
ter has been substituted for *Närrin.*—TR.

CHARLOTTE EMBDEN, HEINE'S ONLY SISTER.

of people marched about the streets singing and making a row, put him in a fever of excitement and made living in the city unbearable. He moved into a country house in a retired quiet neighborhood and with a good air, hoping thereby to obtain some alleviation of his sufferings.

Unfortunately this effect was not obtained, and the poet's health, instead of being improved in Passy, was rather worsened. He wrote in this connection:

LXXVII

PASSY, August 12, 1848.

DEAREST SISTER:

The condition of my eyes is so indifferent that I purchase each letter which I write with my own hand at the cost of the most violent pains, and since you would surely not wish to have a letter at such a price, I shall to-day and hereafter make use of a strange pen in order to impart to you news of my health. It has not in any way improved, but there is no danger present, and the sad thing about it is just this, that I stick to life. So you need not be anxious, but I do deserve pity in the highest degree.

I am often martyred by the most horrible cramps, and at the same time have to sit like a man in chains. For two months I have entirely lost the use of my feet and legs and have to be rolled to and fro on a chair. I have become a miserable paralytic who would be a great burden to you if I were with you. Still, I support myself with the idea of coming to visit you next year, and meantime we have leisure to arrange everything with regard to my comfort. It is not possible this year; I have a thousand things to put in order here, since the revolution and my sudden mishap of paralysis have thrown all my worldly affairs into the most complete confusion. I hope things will get on better, and meantime I bear my fate with patience. My wife loses her head and acts often as if crazed.

I have not yet written to Max, but shall soon. Greet your husband for me and kiss for me my dear nieces. To Ludwig my hearty greeting, and thanks for his loving sympathy.

Your most affectionate brother,

H. HEINE.

LXXVIII

PARIS, September 11, 1848.

DEAR, KIND MOTHERLET:

For five weeks these are the first lines I have written with my own hand. For the sake of my eyes I avoid this entirely, and you too must presently be content if I write you through my secretary. I suffer so much at each letter that on the whole you should be glad that I do not put myself to such painful expense on your account. I wrote you long ago that my right arm also suffers from such cramps as are the forerunners of paralysis.

Otherwise things are as usual; money, cowardly money, which crept away in fear of the Republic, creeps out again into daylight. I go to the city not at all, and take no account of anything but my health. I hope that you and Lotta, as well as the dear children, are in good health! We love you inexpressibly. I shall stay here four weeks longer; the weather is beautiful.

Your faithful son,

H. HEINE.

LXXIX

PARIS, October 19, 1848.

DEAR MOTHER AND DEAREST SISTER:

Just now I received your letter, in which I note with delight your good health. As to myself, my condition is always the same, or else only a very little better. My cramps have let up a little, but my eyes are ridiculously bad, although I spare them in a way hard to describe, never read, and do not write with my own hand even to you. But letters, dear Lotta, I always read with my own eyes, a thing which I state to you particularly because of your questions. As regards the cholera, you need also not worry yourselves at all in my regard; this ancient beast is moreover not so much to be feared as formerly. Matters are more terrible in Vienna, and our poor Gustav may well have suffered some anxiety.

Write me how it has happened with him. I do not correspond directly with him. My wife is in good health, and asks to be warmly remembered to you all. We talk all the time of you all, and particularly concerning mother we can never say enough that is pleasant and agreeable. The main thing that I have to report to you to-day is that I am still very content with my new house, and in nowise rue the sacrifice which I made for the change. We live quietly, retired and safe from bullets. Greet and kiss for me the youthful gossipry and remain affectionately attached

To your true

H. HEINE.

LXXX

PARIS, December 28, 1848.

DEAREST, KIND MOTHER:

Although writing is forbidden me, I cannot help congratulating you at the new year with my own hand. God keep you and grant you still many and happy years. I also congratulate you, dear Lotta. A New Year's cake such as we ate in Düsseldorf in the morning with our coffee, which latter was composed of three beans and three pounds of chicory! No thought of sugar! Do you still recall the old coffeepot that looked like a flowerpot or a Roman vase? Was made of very beautiful black tin.

Farewell, and keep in affection

Your trusty

H. HEINE.

LXXXI

PARIS, March 29, 1849.

DEAR LOTTA:*

Your letter has shaken my nerves grievously and since then I have been crying and crying until to-day I can hardly see at all. Only one word of comfort : dying is no ill luck, but this is— to suffer for years before one can reach the point of dying. Suffering year after year! happy are they who get through with it quickly—*per acquit* as our little father used to say—and one turns round and goes to sleep and everything is paid for!

I am at this moment too much in pain to condole with your husband particularly ; silently I press his hand. And you, poor, strong heart, how much have you had to bear! God preserve you, my dear, kind sister!

You, my dearest mother, will have to wait some time for a letter from me, and to-day I can only hastily embrace you.

Kiss my Lotta and the children for me. My wife is well. I am still in the same wretched state.

Your trusty

H. HEINE.

* On the death of her youngest daughter.

LXXXII

PARIS, April 21, 1849.

DEAR, KIND MOTHER:

I have hoped from day to day to feel better
and am very much annoyed that I have nothing
pleasant to report concerning my state of health.
My eyes seem to grow better, but now I am
suffering again from cramps in the right arm and
in the same hand, which further spoils my writing
terribly. My wife asks to be heartily remembered. The call to her final home of my poor
niece has saddened us inexpressibly and I, who
am now so easily upset, have become sick for
eight days in consequence of the news—a sickness within a sickness! What people can support! And how you must have suffered then,
and must still suffer! God keep you and my
Lotta. I hope that you are in good health; tell
me the truth.

Farewell, and keep in affection

Your trusty

H. HEINE.

LXXXIII

PARIS, June 14, 1849.

DEAREST, KIND MOTHER:

I entreat you to write me soon. I cannot imagine why I am so long without a letter from you. Here we are, living in anxiety and wretchedness. The cholera is raging frightfully. People are falling like flies. My wife is sick too, and I have almost lost my head. I myself am still as sick as a dog, but the cholera spares all the chronic sick, probably because they always live in a regular way. Kiss Lotta and the children for me. My wife asks to be heartily remembered. I hope that you are well. Sickness is the worst of wretchedness; death is the slightest and most easily borne.

Your everlastingly loving, trusty son,

H. HEINE.

LXXXIV

PARIS, August 7, 1849.

DEAR, GOOD SISTER:

Your last letter has saddened me greatly; I can well imagine how much you might have suffered from the agitation in Hamburg because of

the lay of your house. I fear you are oftener con-
fined to your bed than I know ; I pray you tell me
the truth. We live in a period when people have
nothing much that is pleasant to report, and comfort can only be extracted from the certainty that
the unhappiness is as great as we know, so that
imagination does not worry us with uncertainty.

I am getting on as usual, my eyes suffering
terribly, and I am consumed with sorrow and the
feeling of utter helplessness. For that reason I
write you seldom and but little ; but I think of
you almost all the time, and no night passes that
I do not make an offering of tears to you.

Things are as usual with my wife—an angel
who often has devilish whims, and the sweetest
squanderer who ever in this world tortured and
made her husband happy.

I kiss my dear Lotta a thousand times.

Your trusty son,

H. HEINE.

LXXXV

PARIS, August 19, 1849.

DEAR, KIND MOTHERKIN :

I see with terror in the papers how desolate
the outlook is with you and how my friends in

Prussia are carrying on. Were I there, they would certainly nab me on this occasion. Everything is quiet with us, even in my household. My wife, thank God, is of good health and tries to gladden as much as possible my wretched existence. She is a kindly child and if she gives me pain it is not her fault but her disease. God keep her, as well as all of you ; kisses and greetings to dear sister and the children.

You, dear mother, were always an honest, God-fearing woman, of true piety, and for your sake God who is good will always stand us by.

Your trusty son,

H. HEINE.

LXXXVI

PARIS, October 24, 1849.

DEAR, KIND MOTHER :

Just now I have your dear letter ; if you knew how unwillingly I wrote you would not demand a letter from me often. In the first place I am seeing very ill for the last few days and then I have really nothing very fascinating to impart. May the devil fly away with my eyes! all the quackery helps me little. Only to you, dear mother, do I write with my own hand; in your case dictation won't do, since in spite of all some intimate things will slip out.

I congratulate you on your little Viennese nephew; thank God that from this fertility I can at least perceive that Gustav is in good health. Moreover, I see that he is not deceiving his wife!

To-day I can see nothing. That's why I shall write you one of these days, and you get these lines only in order to judge of my good health from them.

Kisses for Lotta.

Your trusty son,

H. HEINE.

Dictation was extremely uncomfortable to Heine, and it took a long while before he accustomed himself to it. He said in this regard : " Heretofore I always wrote everything myself and believe that, especially as regards German, it is a poor affair to dictate prose. The author has to consider carefully not only the stress of tone but also the architectural structure of his periods. Our language is also arranged for the eye; it is plastic, and in rhyming not only the sound but the spelling makes a difference. Singularly enough, the difference which exists in this respect between German and French expresses itself even in the verbal definition of the matter. Germans call their understanding of a thing *Einsicht*, but Frenchmen *entendement*. The German, according to my opinion, must see before him in plastic form what he creates in speech. One can dictate verses made in the head more easily than prose; and I could not do that either; even then I would have to change a great deal."

Heine wrote his manuscript on great folio sheets in big letters with a pencil, as soon as his health permitted, and only dictated his letters.

LXXXVII

PARIS, January 21, 1850.

DEAREST, KIND MOTHER:

I received all right your and dear Lotta's letter with wishes for the New Year. I hope you have entered on this year in pleasant fashion. May Heaven permit it to end quietly and without a scare. In my case the year has not taken on any character yet ; it drones along, idiotic and melancholy like the last.

Not the slightest change in my state of health ; I spare my eyes always, but without result. If I did not spare them even as the apple of my eye, I would be blind now, which is of course the greatest evil from which may a good God preserve one. For that reason I still do not write you by my own hand, but that makes no great difference, since I never express thoughts any more in letters.

My wife is still suffering from the results of her silliness ; she cannot walk yet, but begins to hop about the room now on one leg like a frog. She asks to be remembered with the most heartfelt tenderness, but in general you are our staple of conversation. My wife bears her mishap with less impatience than I expected ; she makes up for the bad moments when her temper is ugly by such an amount of infinite sweetness at other times that I can always find my accounts in this business on the right side. I pray you to write me soon, and from you too I expect a long letter concerning yourself and the darlings—the entire holy family !

I hope you are entirely restored from your mishap. That domestic jester, von Wihl, visits me occasionally and never fails to amuse me in one way or another. To be sure, one must be on one's guard with him ; but, to be sure, who is the person with whom one must not be on one's guard?

Concerning the nonsense in German newspapers on my so-called conversion I will not say anything. In this case it is the same thing as in all the news in the papers about me.

And now, dear mother, farewell. May gracious God preserve you, keep you from pain and eye trouble, spare your dear health, and though things often do not go as you would like, yet comfort yourself with the thought that few women have been loved and worshiped by their children as you have and as verily you deserve to have been, my own dear, honest, upright and true mother! What are all the others in comparison with you?

People ought to kiss the ground your feet have trod.

This winter is infinitely raw—would that you kept warm in that thin, wobbly little dwelling of yours near the Dammthor! I let myself lack for nothing and for warming burn whole forests. Am generally well cared for.

Your faithful son,

H. HEINE.

In the above letter Heine calls it nonsense when German newspapers talk about his conversion; and yet, although perhaps at the time he did not know it himself, a change was taking place in his way of religious thinking.

Heine, who had been brought up in his parents' house to the faith of Israel, was held by those parents to a strict worship of God without any insistance on ritual; but in 1825 he went over to the Lutheran faith. His philosophical studies which occupied him all his life, raised him far above the forms of all positive religions.

Passing forward he reached a poetic pantheism by the way of the new teaching of Saint Simonism. If later he remained always a freethinker, still in the end atheism gave him a disgust, and, sharply tried by the long sufferings of his sick bed, he returned again to pure, formless deism.

LXXXVIII

PARIS, March 15, 1850.

DEAREST MOTHER:

I have duly received the letter in which you note the reception of the bill of exchange; yes, I repeat my promise that I will at once notify you if I should fall into any momentary embarrassment, in order that I may have command of the returned sum of money, which is safer in your hands than in mine. I think I have already told you that on the whole my finances are properly arranged, so that only temporary embarrassments could arise, which are not painful, but merely annoying, and that the next quarterly payment always fills up the deficit of the preceding quarter in the quietest and most regular fashion.

The expenses of my sickness are very large, not because I need physician or apothecary much, but because I have to guard myself by sacrifices of money from many noxious influences.*

But as to my sickness, the worst of all is that

---

* Meaning the financial assistance which Heine gave to many of the German refugees in Paris.

one hangs on to life so long, a thing, dear mother, which naturally does not seem to you the worst ; but I, who have to bear so much physically and lose all hope of cure, I envy people who are quickly snatched away by acute diseases. In death the terrible thing consists only of this : that it plunges our dear ones into woe. How gladly would I leave this world if I did not think of the helplessness of my squanderer, the misery of the old baggage who lives near the Dammthor and the tears of my sister ! I thank her for her latest kind advices. My darling Lotta always gives me the greatest pleasure when I get one of her letters. But you must not expect an answer from me often, for it gives me too much sorrow to find that I can write you only saddening or mournful letters and even these only by a third hand.

I send hearty thanks to my nephew for his friendly letter, which I read with pleasure, but with great difficulty. He must write me often, but with black ink and in legible writing. I am anxious to learn from you how the young fellow will come out and what we may expect from him. I send greeting to Nanny and Nelly and kiss them.   How often I think of my dear Nanny, my sweet child—and about the sweet *Auf-lauf* which she knew so well how to prepare ! * Would I had my Nanny here, together with so well cooked a dish !   After that I would drink a good cup of tea, but not one from the first pouring, but from the last cups, which she used to keep all for herself.

My wife, who is going out walking once more and is in good health, sends her love.

And now farewell.   Keep in affection

Your faithful

H. HEINE.

LXXXIX

PARIS, May 6, 1850.

MY DEAR, KIND MOTHER

AND MUCH BELOVED SISTER :

With joy did I receive the letter, from which I gathered your good health and in which at the same time I find more loving sympathy than I can possibly deserve, more than might seem at times quite to fit me.   How can I repay all this ?

* A sweet dish that rises in the oven like an omelette-soufflée.— TR.

And how can I satisfy your loving wishes always to be kept advertised of my condition in a state of things like this: when every communication with outside, if it must be given in German, is made particularly difficult for me?

For you must know I have no longer the help of the German who for the last twelve years cared for my correspondence, and as I cannot dictate any German to the Frenchman who has taken his place, it is not every day that a German pen is at my command in order to communicate with you. So that if from now on you get letters from me at still more irregular intervals you may put it down to this state of things and absolve me from every blame of unloving neglect.

For the rest, nothing particularly remarkable has taken place here. I feel somewhat better about the heart; I suffer a little less; but I fear that the disease goes always onward with its quiet but fatal snail's pace. I avoid almost all medicine. My wife is in excellent health, is getting very stout, and asks to be affectionately remembered.

Carl comes to see me now and then; he was

four times here in one month, but he appears to
be on the point of leaving on a journey. I touch
on nothing that may hurt his feelings. He has a
good heart; but between heart and pocket there
is no railroad in running order. I do not complain, and always let things go along now as go
they will.

I heartily thank you, dear Lotta, for the
kindly eagerness to serve me; but in this regard
I refer to what long ago I told dear mother. Is
it not possible to send German books to me here
from your circulating library and by the steamer
which might also bring them back?

I would like now and then to have some German piece read aloud to me, and as I never get
from the bookseller here the volume I ask for,
and as there is no circulating library here, I must
look about me for an escape. In case it can be
done, you might send me a catalogue from Hamburg under separate cover.

I do not go into the country, but nevertheless
I shall, and no later than to-morrow, perform
something extremely idyllic: I shall begin to
drink ass's milk! My physician has ordered it—
and if it is wholesome for me I shall gladly take

refuge among the donkeys.* I should have
written to Gustav long ago if I had not again
lost his address. But I shall write to him presently to ask him to do something for me in
Vienna; so send me his address again. I have
had the most affectionate letter from Max.

The idea of transporting myself with my household to Hamburg often bobs up in my mind, and
if I were sure that this transfer and the bang and
bounce would not attack my poor body too much,
it might at last come to be carried out. Unfortunately I am up to my ears in work and although
it strains me much, I can't avoid all business and
all literary work. Write me soon and much.

If Ludwig can get away from Hamburg one of
these days for a little while without neglecting in
any way his business, it might be well to take advantage of the present quickness and cheapness
of railway travel and send him to Paris just for
once. I would see him here with the greatest
pleasure and might make use of him through advice and commissions by word of mouth which

* A favorite in that menagerie of beasts which Germans use as
synonyms of stupidity. See " Die Wahlesel," a political satire,
vol. iii. p. 219.—TR.

would also be very profitable for my most intimate affairs. Everything would be finished in eight days and the boy would have had no leisure to get too exact an acquaintance with Paris.

And now farewell; keep me in affection: write to me much, especially on family matters, and forgive me if I keep you waiting long for answers. I greet my nephew Ludwig heartily, and so with all the rest.

I would like some day a letter, and moreover in her own handwriting, from my dear niece Anna. She need not bother herself a bit, and may write whatever comes into her head. I have a good cook now, but a regular *Auflauf* with sweetmeats cannot be made in France as it is with you in the North.

God pour much happiness and blessing, dear Lotta, upon your new house!

Your faithful
H. HEINE.

XC

PARIS, June 15, 1850.

DEAREST MOTHER:

I have duly received your kind letter, with postscripts by Lotta and Nanny, and would have

written you sooner if it had not been for the
difficulties concerning German correspondence
of which I notified you in my former letter.
Otherwise nothing has happened, and as regards
my illness, it puts me out a great deal if I have
to sing to you, dear mother, my old song of complaint with the same old sorrowful variations.
I will only repeat: the worst of this illness is
that one merely suffers frightfully from it, but
does not die quickly. You can rest assured that
I shall not conceal any turn for the worse. If I
do not write, you need imagine nothing more
than that I have not at hand a friendly penman,
or else that I do not wish to blacken still more
my already sufficiently darkened mood by sorrowful communications to you. But I think of
you constantly; be assured of that. Truth to
say, I would like to survive you in order to spare
you the sorrow of the news of my death—and
perhaps that is now the chief interest I take in
life. When I no longer have you I shall turn
toward death with a much lighter heart. Lotta
has her children and husband, and so far as my
wife is concerned, she has too happy a nature
that she could not in the long run do without me.

Don't you perceive how much reason I have not to write often—only melancholy funeral-call letters! I have turned into a very sorrowful, fun-lacking clown!

Thank you, dear sister, for having considered my hastily expressed desire in regard to books. But I told you that you should send me under separate cover a catalogue. Such a sending would have cost eight shillings at the most. Instead of that, Jovien the bookseller has sent me his catalogue in a parcel by way of Havre, and added to said parcel three more books, which have not the slightest interest for me. I am sending you these books by hand of Carl Heine presently; he takes them with him and in that way saves me the expenditure of seven francs, for that is what the parcel costs, since the rascals of forwarding agents in Havre charge just as much commission and costs for the couple of books as for a large box; the freight itself, particularly from Havre hither, is very unimportant. But I would gladly pay such a sum for parcels of books which have some interest for me in the reading, and if I find no occasion to send them back, will return them quickly at my own expense. But in order that I may not need to repeat this too often, I must beg that at least a dozen books be sent me at once, and that nothing be sent which I did not expressly ask for.

Among the books which I wish to read are the writings of Dickens (Boz), especially his "Pickwick" and travels in America and Italy. "Humphrey's Clock" by the same author, as well as his "Cricket on the Hearth," I have already read. Then I would like the writings of Gogol translated from the Russian. Moreover I wish to read a novel by L. Storch which is called in the catalogue: "The Star of Jacob, a Messiad." If this book is not on hand, I would like to read the following numbers by that author. Many of Tieck's novels also I have not read and I beg you to send the volumes marked. Look, dear Lotta, and see if there is not in the circulating library the first and second parts of "Die Kronen-wächter," by Arnim, the latter volume of which only appeared a few years ago.* Enough for the present!

Some of these will doubtless be found, from

* L. Achim von Arnim, a writer of romances and short stories, who is still read in Germany.—TR.

which as soon as possible a neat invoice can be put together, but I pray you to let them come soon, since I find occasion oftener in summer to send back the books without expense.

I send my heartiest thanks for her letter to my dear niece Anna; I would have infinite pleasure in seeing her again, for everybody tells me so much that is nice and delightful concerning her. If she turns out like her mother and grandmother, the husband may congratulate himself who ends by bagging her, particularly if she also has the gentleness of both.

Your loving, faithful

H. HEINE.

XCI

PARIS, June 18, 1850.

DEAREST, KIND MOTHER:

I hope that these lines find you in good condition; on my side, for the last two days I feel better than usual, because with nervous disorders such as mine conditions change so, that one despairs to-day and rejoices again the day after and never knows where one's health exactly stands. It is this lack of stability which furnishes the reason why I never give you details concerning my sufferings, which are certain to have changed by the time you have received my letter.

Carl Heine is about to leave, and so I send by him back to Hamburg the books of the circulating library. In my last letter day before yesterday I forgot to remark that I am also acquainted with that one of the works of Boz (Dickens) which is entitled "Christmas Tale," and that therefore you need not send it to me. Moreover I forgot to remark that Mr. Jovien has given my address wrong, and for that reason his parcel took long to find me. Therefore Lotta must give him my correct address for the sending of books, which I expect as soon as possible. My wife is in good health, but unfortunately she becomes more corpulent every day. She weighs 180 pounds already. She asks to be heartily remembered to you, and never ceases to talk about you all.

This morning the world-renowned poet Wihl made me a visit and commissioned me to impart his compliments to my mother and sister. Barring his vanity, which might cause him to do the worst of things, and certainly has lured him to much that is evil, he is, all the same, a very kind person.

I have not yet reached the point of writing to Gustav, as every epistolary communication in German, as you know, is made hard for me; but I shall write to him soon, as I have some commissions for him to be executed in my interests and am sure of his love for me. You, dear Lotta, I heartily greet, as well as my dear nieces and nephews also.

Tell me, dear Lotta, why I get no letter from Campe. My drafts are punctually paid by him every time I draw on him for my quarterly pension, but I get no answer to any of my letters. What does he want? What is he cooking up? Luckily, I have no need at present to publish anything; otherwise this silence on his part, which might force me to enter into relations with other publishers, would put me to some embarrassment. But he can hardly know that, and this absence of reply on his part admits of no reply. Try to find out something in this connection, my dear Lotta, and write me in general as much as you can.

Your faithful

H. HEINE.

XCII

PARIS, July 25, 1850.

DEAREST MOTHER:

My last letter crossed yours and it is probable that this will happen again. I hope that you are all well—which is the main thing. On my side, I am feeling so-so, and even though my sickness is still not dwindling, nevertheless it seems to me as if my strength were gaining, and there are days in which I feel little pain and permit my fancy a free course with wide-flying plans of health. I work little, but my mind was never more alert, active and robust. Things are still bad as regards my eyes. Again I have tried to write, but it went ill with me. In order not to blot so much I often write with the lead pencil, which is however very cumbersome.

My dear Lotta has my hearty greeting and thanks for the advices she sends. I have received the books, but am in poor luck with this consignment, for on the one hand I have got things which do not please me entirely and yet were things I wanted; on the other hand I have received what I have read already, perhaps because I do not express myself properly. Now it shall be my care to find an occasion to send the books back again soon. I would like to know whether the costs would be less if I caused the books to be brought by rail direct from Hamburg; Ludwig should make inquiry whether in any event one can send parcels directly hither by the trains and how much freight must be paid for a given number of pounds. All I know is that parcels which come here from Cologne by rail only cost a ridiculously small amount.

My wife asks to be remembered heartily; we talk of you day and night, mostly at night, for we never go to bed earlier than twelve or one o'clock. We live quietly and in the greatest unity, and never was my wife more reasonable than just now. And yet the Germans here have spread a report that I am separated from my wife on account of quarrels. You have no conception what sort of vermin crawls about here under the name of Germans. The person against whom Lotta warns me is nevertheless quite a precious stone by comparison with the louse from whom Campe pretends to have received news of me and whom he calls Ferdinand W. A wretch, to whom for fifteen years I have shown kindnesses, and who nevertheless at last performed such low tricks that I was forced to turn him out in disgrace!

I repeat, dear mother, that I am getting on better; perhaps I am somewhat unjust, as all sick folk are, and will not acknowledge to myself that I am at least twenty-four per cent. better in health than before.

And now farewell; write me soon and a good deal, and keep in affection,

Your faithful

H. HEINE.

XCIII

PARIS, August 3, 1850.

DEAREST, KIND MOTHER:

I hope that you are in a good state of health and that I shall soon get letters from you in which I shall see this hope confirmed. I hasten to-day to notify you before the post leaves that I am sending you a parcel of books by the diligence, and pray you to deliver it without delay to Jovien, the keeper of the circulating library,

together with the accompanying list, from which
he may see what books he is to send me at once
by diligence. I expressly say diligence—nothing
by the Hamburg steamer, which I find to-day
will cost more ! For I have been able to express
the present parcel only as far as Aix-la-Chapelle
and, think of it ! the freight that far only costs
two francs ! I beg you will therefore tell me
how much you had to pay for the package from
Aix to Hamburg, not only in order to return
you the money on occasion, but to learn in
general how much the freight is by land in con-
tradistinction to steamer costs. I beg you also
not to forget to let the bookseller know that he is
to send the books off without delay.

I greet heartily my dear Lotta, and hope that
my dear sister will write me soon and much.
I live very isolated, and otherwise would not
hear anything about Hamburg affairs.

No change has taken place in my health ; I
bear my lot quietly and enjoy the finest household peace—as well as cherry tarts, which my
cook knows how to bake in a very superior
fashion. My cook is a female genius, and under
the title of German *Nudeln* she constructs a dish

which is actually the *schalet** of the Jews, the
which I eat with pleasure. There is the greatest
bit of news I have to impart!

Farewell, and keep me in affection.

Your faithful son,
H. Heine.

XCIV

Paris, September 26, 1850.

Dear, Kind Mother

  and Much Beloved Sister:

Since my last letter nothing much that is en-
joyable has occurred; my health is just the same,
but my household arrangements, as I foresaw,
have turned much more annoying. The young
girl of whom I wrote you has become seriously
ill, and as I did not have the heart to send her
away, I now have two sick people in my house.
For the last six weeks she has been bedridden,
will not be able to convalesce very quickly, and
the physician makes but small promise for the
future. Her illness comes from poor blood; she

---

*A fruit cake like shortcake, perhaps originally the same term
as charlotte, and if so of unknown origin. Some Jews claim
schalet as the original. Called by Polish Jews *schlod.*—Tr.

is as good as lost, and from this direction I may expect a great deal that is unpleasant. On the one hand my wife loses her factotum and a necessary companion for walking in the streets, and I lose my caretaker and reader in French, who was at my orders every hour. I now have someone to read French to me in the evening only, and have been placed under the necessity of hiring a *garde malade,* who bores me greatly by her lazy, negligent ways, who consumes a great deal of feed, is black of complexion and —costs me notwithstanding 150 francs a month ; that is to say, five francs a day. For this reason my wife is very naturally not always in a happy mood, and you can easily see that under these circumstances I often yearn for you. But at present I must not yet think of emigrating to Hamburg: at least not until my health has taken on more solid strength, by which I mean that the cramps from which I suffer a great deal must first stop.

As I have always told you, my disease is a painful, nervous one, and in its case every movement becomes unbearable. I might put my body in danger during a transfer to Hamburg, moreover it is not certain that the climate there would suit me at present.

You see how cautiously and forethoughtfully I go to work, and how it will not be my fault if the bankruptcy of my body should set in at least before you, my dear mother, are at rest.

We talk of you here all the time and I can assure you that my wife does not spare any trouble in caring for me. She sends hearty greetings to you, as well as to the younger generation. Tell my nephew Ludwig that his cousin Drucker has written me a very nice letter and sent me a catalogue; but in this catalogue there is even less to be found than in the Hamburg catalogue, and I don't know yet whether I can make any use of it. For the present I shall stick to Hamburg, but I must beg that I shall not be kept waiting so long for the dispatch of books. Yesterday I sent the last invoice back by express and addressed once more to dear mother in Hamburg. You will have to pay a larger freight this time than in the last instance, because I could not frank it even to the frontier.

A stupid fellow, to whom I committed the forwarding of the package, did not even bring me back a receipt from the post, and so you must let me know at once if the books have arrived in good order. I don't know whether you still possess the former list of books which I sent you latterly; for greater certainty I shall give you inclosed once more the list of books I wish to have. Particularly care for this, however: that the package be sent at once, and that I shall not have to wait so long; moreover be careful that the correct street number gets on the address, as well as a small estimate of value.

I thank you much for your last letter, and particularly you, dear Lotta, must I thank for all your communications and funny passages.

If there is a good circulating library in Hamburg beside that of Jovien, then send me a catalogue of it under separate cover.

Your faithful

H. HEINE.

XCV

PARIS, November 23, 1850.

DEAREST, KIND MOTHER:

I hope that you are in good health, and that the terrible winter approaching may not shake you. At every increase of this raw weather I ever think of you, your dear, weak body, the miserable rotten roof of your old abode near the Dammthor, and every blast of wind which you must feel there; and my heart is often in deeper anxiety than you can conceive. You would do well, therefore, to write me often nowadays.

As regards myself, no changes have taken place in my condition; I am always hoping that things will be better, and every morning this hope turns out a liar. What shall I do? I must take life even as God gives it me. I permit nothing to lack in caretaking, and my wife is happy if she can spend the last sous for the expenses of my sickness and the improvement of my condition.

With regard to the maid, I had a hard battle with her (Mathilde) before I persuaded her to send the poor creature to the hospital, where she actually is at present, and already finds herself noticeably better. Had I done this four months ago, not only would I be richer by a notable sum of money, but I would have escaped certain costly false positions, from which I can extract myself with difficulty only now—I am speaking with regard to my domestics. Many an old tangled spot on my finances seems now to get light upon it, and I have a prospect of rescuing at last something of a good many matters already given up for lost. What has annoyed me most is, that I am not in a position to earn a sous at a time when I might do so much.

Again not a word from Campe, whose silence appears to be calculated for this end: to await the moment when I am "blowing at the last hole" and must give myself up, bound hand and foot, for an apple and a bit of bread! He is mistaken. I wrote to Gustav not long ago and burdened him with some literary commission.

Although my dear Lotta writes that the little chest with books was sent from Hamburg hither as early as October 2, nevertheless up to to-day I have never received it and pray Lotta to make the necessary inquiries. I confess that I am not a little grumpy over this.

And now farewell; I kiss you all truly and heartily.

H. HEINE.

No improvement had occurred in Heine's paralytic condition and the extremities of his body remained without movement.

In the morning after a lukewarm bath he was carefully removed from his bed to an invalid's chair stuffed with soft blankets, for the slightest pressure and every quick movement caused the most violent pains to his suffering body. He once called out to his physician, who was once present at this transfer: "Now you can see how people in Paris worship me and fairly *dandle me on their hands !* "

At night a maid had to sleep near him and by his special command his wife's chamber was placed as far as possible away from his own in order to spare her night rest.

The ordering of his household was that of a well to do burgher residence and the extravagant decorations of modern luxury were absent. His bedchamber, always roomy and airy, made a homelike impression despite its simplicity ; beyond the absolutely necessary objects were a few seats near his bed for visitors and opposite these a writing table covered with a countless mass of papers, journals and books. The reception room was furnished with red satin furniture, the walls were embellished with a portrait of his wife, an oil likeness of his sister, a lithographic portrait of Salomon Heine, and a little bookshelf filled for the most part with his own works in undecorative bindings. In the middle of the room stood a table with albums, books and pictures and on the chimney-piece a bronze time-piece between two porcelain vases which at all times were filled with fresh flowers.

In the morning Heine ate a nourishing break-fast consisting of some light roasted meat, fruits and a glass of Bordeaux and water. After a little rest he began to work, dictated to his secretary, or had someone read aloud. In the afternoon if his health permitted, the poet received the visits of friends, strangers and also of elegant women of the upper classes, whose presence always brightened him up if they were young and pretty. Heine called women " the great nation, ruler of the world."

At six o'clock dinner was taken, which was prepared in a simple but nourishing way, had always variety to offer, and was for the most part eaten with a good appetite. His wife had hard work satisfying his gastronomical demands : for Heine was a great *gourmand* who once said, after a rich banquet at the Café Véfour : " That dinner was so good it deserved to be eaten on one's knees."

Mathilde also loved to eat at the restaurant, and in order to make it possible she often took refuge in the following stratagem. The taste of mutton was very displeasing to her husband ; so, when he asked what there was to eat, as he came home with a good appetite and in a good humor, she would say mutton ! At once he would take up his hat and say : " Come, Mathilde, let us go and dine at Véfour's." If acquaintances were met with on the road they were asked to come along and as Mathilde regarded champagne as a spice which could not be omitted from a good dinner, this joke, being often repeated, caused very considerable expenditures.

XCVI

PARIS, December 2, 1850.

DEAR, KIND MOTHER :

Your dear letter in which you impart to me the confinement of Mme, Gustav Heine, as well as

the little letter from sister, in which she gives
me news of the misunderstandings which have happened as to the books, was duly received last week
and first I shall answer the last with a few lines.

I have done you injustice, dear Lotta, by
charging you with neglectfulness when I did
not get the books from Hamburg which I desired. At that time I received a letter from
young Drucker who informed me that he had
made arrangements with the Schlosschen circulating library to send me parcels of books whenever I forwarded the numbers in the catalogue
which he had sent me under separate cover.
I received this catalogue and at the same time
answered young Drucker and authorized the contract he had made with the Schlosschen circulating library; I sent him at the same time a list
of books which I wanted sent to me.

So, a few days later, when I received these
books, and to the question if they came from
Cologne received from the postman an affirma-
tive answer, I was absolutely certain that these
were the books which I had ordered there; and
after I had had them read aloud to me, I gave
the order to send them back to Cologne to the

Schlosschen circulating library well packed up, and this was duly done under frank, since, as I now perceive, one can prepay parcels as far as Cologne. Along with the package went a letter of directions from me, as the custom is with expressage, and in a separate letter I wrote to the said library such directions as were necessary in regard to a second invoice and as to the money for the books and costs. Now I am indignant that from Cologne, where they must have perceived my error at once, I have received no notification concerning it, and as I don't want to write to the circulating library, which in any case has acted discourteously, nor to the idiotic fellow who was guilty of the botherment, I therefore pray you, dear Lotta, to get Ludwig to write to Cologne, so that the package may be sent to you in Hamburg without delay, and so you can give back the books to the library.

Far more important, dear mother, is the matter concerning which I must enlighten you to-day. But in this case I can be more concise and need not heap up words. I promised you, you will recall, to knock at your door in case I should need the sum of money which you offered me, and unfortunately I must fulfill my promise to-day.   But I wish that you would forward the money to me in the following way : send me at once a bill of exchange for six hundred francs payable here and keep meanwhile the other four hundred francs until I write you when and how you are to send them to me.   I am assuming that you can deprive yourself at present of the money, and as I long ago reported quite frankly the budget of my income, you will not be disquieted, because I would rather ask aid of you than undertake negotiations and moves on account of a small sum which I need at the close of the year, moves which would be costly or disagreeable.   I shall not tell you more, and I hope you trust to my truthfulness; otherwise it will have pained me greatly to have written to you to-day.

No alteration has taken place in my health, but when the change of weather is passed I hope for a certain betterment such as I always experience in winter.

And now farewell, and keep in affection

Your faithful son,

H. HEINE,

50 Rue Amsterdam.

XCVII

PARIS, February 5, 1851.

DEAR, KIND MOTHER AND DEAR SISTER:

I have yet to thank you for your good wishes for the new year; the young brood also I heartily thank. I am rejoiced to see that you all are well. Meanwhile nothing important has happened here. I am again in sickly mood, somewhat better than before, perhaps very much better. But I still have severe nerve pains and, unhappily, the cramps draw upward oftener and that tries my head very much. So I now have to bear what God has laid upon me, and I support my lot with patience while I constantly think of you all with love ; moreover I am treated by my wife at this moment with the most tender care ; nothing that my nursing requires is omitted, nor anything that can procure me pleasure or the assuagement of pain.

My finances also are at this moment exceedingly well arranged and in this regard Carl also has put me under obligations, since this year, of his own movement and without preliminary bang and bounce, he has given me the needful sums. I do not so much as trouble myself to think from what direction this favorable treatment arises, even as I shall in general neither worry nor rejoice in this world concerning aught that relates to money. May God's will be done !

And then I cannot take complete care beforehand for the squanderer. She is too lovable and her faults arise too much from goodness of heart that I could grumble at her for even the most senseless expenditures and such like follies. Without her would not life be devoid of interest? She helps me support this painful burden which I certainly would throw aside were I alone in the world.

Write to me very soon ; and you, dear Lotta, do give me as many details as possible. I thank you for the books you attended to, which I shall probably send back to-morrow to Hamburg to mother's address.

As I can prepay only a short distance, you, dear mother, must again pay a large expressage for me, but you perform a great favor by so doing. For the circulating library at Cologne contains but few books which I can use and so I can draw thence little that is enlivening. The catalogue at

Hamburg is much richer, and despite the larger cost, dear Lotta, I must therefore beg that you will cause a new invoice to reach me thence, and that as soon as possible! For this purpose I send you the inclosed list; if, contrary to expectation, so many books are out on loan that enough volumes cannot be forwarded, I beg nevertheless that this invoice be not filled up with books that I have not put down on the list. I depend on it however, and beg you to inform me when the volumes have been dispatched.

Farewell and keep in hearty affection

Your faithful

H. HEINE.

XCVIII

PARIS, March 12, 1851.

DEAREST, KIND MOTHER:

I was most uncommonly delighted to receive your last letter. A few days before I had received a few lines from Lotta, and in the letter found not a single word from you. At the same time I had an epistle from Mr. Wirth,* who

* Georg Wirth, introduced to Heine by Spiller von Hauenschild (Max Waldau), a merchant of remarkable literary cultivation.

began with a statement that he had not been able to see you because you were not in good health.   Anyone else would have worried himself to death, but after serious consideration I was able to quiet my mind by acknowledging to myself that Lotta would not have written any joyous letters if it were a serious illness, but that in such a case one would express one's self with different turns of phrase and with a certain embarrassment.   I hope, therefore, that you, dear mother, are well.   But if by chance it should be the case that you are seriously ill, tell me frankly ; for the whole truth is not so torturing as doubt.

Things are better with me, but move very slowly. For two years I have taken no medicine, or rather my wife won't suffer any more that a bottle of medicine shall cross the threshold ; and all the doctors too she has sent packing to the devil, with the exception of a single one, whom I do not see for months at a time and who is of so minute a size that really I may almost say I employ no doctor at all.*

Among a number of ills one should always choose the least.

Nevertheless I do not believe that I shall ever

* Dr. Gruby, a Hungarian.

stand on sound legs again. I am done with this world and if I were sure that some time I should be received with affability in heaven I would bear my existence in patience.

My greatest happiness is to think of you, dear mother, of Lotta, my brothers and the little brood. My wife conducts herself in an almost exemplary fashion. She eases me and makes my life beautiful. She comforts and delights me, but now and then unwittingly breaks my heart with her irreclaimable squandering. There is no help for this; that is really my greatest chagrin. Her fever to be constantly pouring out money is frightful. And at the same time I am no miser. Long ago I stopped laughing about it.

I send hearty greeting to my dear Lotta. Mr. Wirth who called on her, is a very nice and extraordinarily talented, not to say a most honest and upright person; I myself have but little acquaintance with him, but know him well through friends in common.

The books whose dispatch Lotta announces have not yet arrived, and I hope that there will not be great botherations with them again. Herr Wirth can tell Campe as he will what I

said to him. Lotta was in error when she believed it necessary to forbid him so to do. But
to have something said by a third person purposely is a thing that does not suit me ; I have
always found that not much salvation came to
me from such circumlocution ; I speak out everything that I desire people should know, but I
cannot afford to bring myself down to the level
of making anybody my *compère*.

My wife asks to be remembered heartily to you
all ; entire days are spent by us in talking about
you, dear mother and about Lotta. She has
not forgotten a word of all that Lotta said, and
our conversation always ends with this—I have
to show her my tongue !

Do write me lots and soon, for I live retired
from the whole world and it might happen
profitably to me to be particularly *au fait* in
family matters. And you, dear Lotta, are you in
good health ? Don't you think you could show
me your tongue by way of the electric telegraph?
I greet your husband heartily, as well as the
young folks. To the younger ladies, greetings
at your convenience.

With love and faithfulness,

H. HEINE.

XCIX

PARIS, June 7, 1851.

DEAR, KIND MOTHER:

Again a long time has elapsed since I have
had news of your good health. I hope that you
have withstood well the transition season; it has
prickled me a bit; but, as I imagine, I have
escaped in sounder case than last year. My
condition has improved a little, though at the
same time there is still much occasion for complaint remaining. It has saddened me that
Gustav has given up his journey hither for the
moment, owing to overmuch work. I have a
great many visits from Germans, but they rarely
have anything pleasant to impart. Yesterday I
learned the scandalous history which has compromised the Gabes in your town and the whole
Oppenheim family. I mean the locking up of
the Gabes mother owing to alleged insanity.
The woman is here now and everyone who hears
her adventure is outraged.*

Is it really true that Dr. S. has hanged him-

* There appeared at the time a pamphlet on the subject, "A
Mother in the Insane Asylum."

self? I beg Lotta to tell me something more
particular about it; I can hardly believe it.
Things are beginning to look very melodramatic
in our family! * * *

I received the books long ago, and shall send
them back again one of these days with hearty
thanks.   Hearty greetings to Lotta, the children,
and Ludwig: the last I have yet to thank for his
recent letter.

What you write me with regard to Dr. Halle,
dear Lotta, is proof of your sympathetic heart;
I, too, feel great interest in the fate of the
remarkable man, but miserliness may have
readily added a good deal to his monomania.
Latterly I was visited by the head of the banking
house Warschan in Königsberg, who is related
to John F. in Berlin, and he told me in confidence that the latter was also nearly insane;
that he was ever lamenting how in his last days
he would have to starve for lack of money.

I am still without news of Campe.   It stands
to reason, dear mother, that you do not place
any faith in the clack which the German
papers make concerning the condition of my
health.

During these days, dear mother, I have been more occupied with you than you can have dreamed; for I have undertaken a general revision of my papers and have again looked through all your letters and Lotta's, and, however it pained me, have given up all these epistles to the flames in order to be certain that no bad use shall be made of them through some chance breach of trust. I am of sure hope, dear mother, that you agree with this action, since for no consideration on earth would I be willing to expose you to the rude curiosity of persons in the generation to come.

Keep me in warm affection and write to me soon.

Your faithful

H. HEINE.

C

PARIS, July 9, 1851.

DEAREST MOTHER AND DEAR SISTER:

At this moment I am pretty well in health, but I suffered badly with my eyes during the great heat. As I perceive, you have the parcel of books back again; but as I could prepay only

for a few stations, it surely cost you a great deal
of freight. I send you inclosed a new list of
books among which are a few which I wish
very specially to read, for instance, the novel
by Frau von Palzow entitled " St. Roche," and
a novel by Mügge called " Toussaint Louver-
ture."

Here's that stupid fellow Schiff,* who has published " Luftschlösser," a book that is not in the
catalogue, but which I would much like to read.
Everything the stupid fellow writes is good and
exceedingly remarkable ; and he has more talent
than countless other people who have renown.
So it is in literature too—luck is everything.

Dear Lotta, read a book which has appeared
with Campe called " Schief Levinchen und
Mariandel seine Kalle "; it is a masterpiece,
artistic and clever, and I believe it is by Schiff.

---

* Dr. H. Schiff, a stepcousin ; Heine's grandfather married a
widow Schiff in second nuptials. Schiff was a talented author,
but never received the recognition which, according to Heine's
verdict, he deserved. Having got down in the world through
drink, he was given up for hopeless by the family and died in the
Hamburg Hospital. Owing to his friendship with Strodtmann
there arose in the latter's biography of Heine, through statements
made by Schiff, a great many inexact and wrong statements concerning the private and family relations of the poet.

As I hear, dear Lotta, you are entertaining the idea of getting for me the "Geschichte der Komischen Litteratur" by Flögel; I therefore hasten to notify you that some time ago I had it procured and therefore do not need it.

Mr. Wirth has sent me word that Campe is about to visit me here in Paris this month; don't let him notice anything if he does not tell you himself; yet on this occasion I might well avail myself of the chance to have the books brought here by Campe. The young man of whom you made note has not yet appeared at my house and you can be assured that I have understood entirely your meaning. Unhappily I have to burn my dear Lotta's joyous letters at once; nevertheless I must not omit it.

My dear Nanny might often write to me when she does not have too much to do ; this correspondence would certainly be most pleasurable to me. I send regards to Ludwig and Lena too. As for my dear mother, whom I love more than all the cats in the world, I kiss her twenty-five times. My wife sends greetings and perspires.

Your faithful son and brother,

H. HEINE.

Heine felt bitterly hurt by the moody silence of his publisher and very likely it had come to a break with Campe if the latter had not suddenly come to Paris, urged by his own interests, when he learned through Mr. Georg Wirth that the poet had finished a large book notwithstanding his sickly state. Heine intended to issue this work, the " Romanzero," only after death ; but he gave up this resolve at the urgent request of Campe, and the latter bought the work for the sum of six thousand marks. When his own interest was at stake Campe could be extremely pleasant and at the first meeting knew how to change the poet's mood to his own profit. Before the agreement as to price Campe had not examined at all the contents of the manuscript and when Heine asked him how he could pay a notable price for a book without having first read it, he replied : " That is unnecessary; what Heine writes is fine." The poet was by no means unimpressionable by flattery of that kind and this imperturbable trust in the creations of his brain was enough to strengthen once more the somewhat loosened bond of friendship with his publisher.

CI

PARIS, August 21, 1851.

DEAREST, KIND MOTHER:

I duly received your last letter. I have no great opinion of homeopathy, but next year I shall certainly do something important for my health, for I shall make a visit to the baths of Gastein and on this occasion probably go by way of Hamburg. For more than two years now I have taken no medicine. My state of health improves very slowly, but the improvement is not to be ignored.

The arrival of Gustav was a great pleasure to me; for the last six days he has been here with his wife and toward the end of next week he journeys home by way of Hamburg. So he will tell you much about me by word of mouth, and to you also, dear Lotta, he will impart by word of mouth everything which I have to say to you. During the coming weeks I can write but little, since my German secretary lives in the country and very rarely comes to Paris for an hour. Besides this, you can easily believe that I would dictate a letter to you

through very few of the Germans here who sometimes help me out with a pen.

Perhaps I shall send to Campe by Gustav the
entire manuscript of a book, and this can probably be printed in two months. Gustav's arrival
has excited me very much and I shall probably
be capable of no work for a fortnight; we clack
from morning till night. We laugh all the
time and my wife laughs with us; my parrot
screams in between without either of them understanding what the talk is about. My wife finds
that Gustav has a strong resemblance to me.

At this moment Gustav has the pleasure of
learning that the vagabond with whom he recently had a lawsuit in Vienna, the editor of a
rival paper, is to be presently bidden to leave
Vienna.

And now farewell; greet Ludwig, Lena and
Anna, the last of whom I heartily thank for her
gay letter.

Your faithful

H. HEINE.

After Campe's departure Heine was surprised
by the arrival of his brother Gustav, who had

come to Paris with his wife for a visit of a short period. The best understanding existed between the brothers, and many a jocose remark was exchanged between the two.

On his brother's question whether it was really true that he had married a sister of charity Heine answered : "No, rather have I become a monk, and pray God every day that he may impart to you, dear brother, better political views."

To Gustav's demand whether he should not pronounce himself openly in the *Fremdenblatt* concerning his religious change of views Heine rejoined : "What possible difference can it make to the big white elephant of the King of Siam if a wee little mouse in the Rue d'Amsterdam at Paris believes or does not believe in his grandeur and wisdom?"

On his departure Heine gave his brother Gustav the manuscript of the "Romanzero," who brought it to Campe in Hamburg. To the vexation of Heine this meeting unfortunately produced fresh misunderstandings and quarrels with his publisher. In October, a few months later, appeared the "Romanzero," which added new sprays to the poet's laurels.

It was generally considered a marvel that Heine was able to create this clever work during the frightful tortures of his sick bed and preserve unweakened his strength of mind and poetic fire.

Almost at the same time with the " Romanzero" appeared " Der Doctor Faust," a *Tanzpoem*, to which were added later in his miscellaneous works the pantomime-libretto " Die Göttin Diana " and " Die Götter in Exil."*

CII

PARIS, December 5, 1851.

DEAREST MOTHER:

As the greatest excitement is abroad in Paris at this moment, and yesterday and day before yesterday much bloodshed occurred, I hasten to report to you that I am in excellent health and beyond the reach of every danger. At least this advantage exists in my sickness : I do not mix in the combat of partisans. If I had been well I might at this moment have had the chance to be wounded or even shot to death.

* These three pieces are found in vol. viii. of the library edition. —TR.

Unfortunately, at every sound of tumult my wife cannot refrain from sticking her nose out on the street and yesterday was caught in the middle of musketry fire. Unhappily I have no commands at all to give in France, and as in every part of the country, the needful authority is lacking in my abode.

I fear that things are still going ill with Louis Napoleon. Unluckily he has not grasped the fact that the French, it is true, do not love the Republic but still wish to hold on to it. A thing is not readily surrendered which has been won at such cost.

How many people, are there not? who feel resentment to their mistress but still cannot make up their mind to forsake the woman for whom they have spent so much money!

I have received the little box of books, and thank you for the invoice. I hope that the list, which was not sent back to me, has not gone astray; answer me on this point. I have had a letter from Gustav; he writes that he loves his wife very much. Unfortunately I perceive that he has not carried out my business in the way he made me believe he would, and in this con-

néction I fear I shall reap a harvest of new vexations.

I told you in my last letter that I had paid back
everything to Gustav ; nor do I doubt that you
have felt why I mention such things. I am a
sick man, and the hour might easily arrive in
which speech may be impossible.

I greet you heartily, dear Lotta ; remember me
to your husband and kiss my two nieces and my
nephew, whom we always recall here with great
love. My squanderer has bought her a green dress
which I call the Vitzliputzli gown.* For I have
calculated that the gown will cost as much as
the money earned by the poem " Vitzliputzli "
which is found in the " Romanzero." We live in
the most perfect harmony, in the loveliest, cost-
liest peace ! We often talk of you all and often
clack till midnight about dear mother. When
Nanny writes I pray her to take very black ink,
since I always read my family letters myself and
in winter particularly my eyes are very weak.

The " Romanzero " excites more enthusiasm

---

* Referring to his poem which alludes to the old Mexican god of
war of that name, whose symbol is the humming bird with its neck
of brilliant, changing green. See vol. iii. pp. 61–76.—TR.

than I expected. I assure you it is a very weak book; but you must not repeat that. I wrote it with my powers lamed.

I hope, dear mother, that you are very well, and I shall always arrange my health according to yours. You know what I mean.

Write to me soon and much.

Your faithful son,

H. HEINE.

Heine was no worshiper of Napoleon III and as early as 1849 uttered the following:

"A *coup d'état* is an open secret. People gossip so much about it that they end by no longer believing in it ; but it is not going to stay away. The President is working on the model of his uncle and marches on to an eighteenth Brumaire. Up, then, and at it !

" When the Republic was proclaimed about a year ago, the world obtained the impression that something which was nothing but a dream and ought to be a dream only had become a reality. But I have the unhappiness to know France only too exactly through my residence here for years, and I am not at all in the dark concerning what we have to expect.

" The Republic is nothing more than a change
of name, a revolutionary title. How in the world
could this corrupt, effeminate society change so
quickly? To make money, seize on offices, ride
in a coach and four, own a box at the theater
and to chase from one pleasure to another—that
was their ideal hitherto. Where could these fellows have so carefully hidden away their stock of
civic virtues? Believe me, Paris is thoroughly
Napoleonist—I mean that here is the rule of the
Napoleon d'or."*

CIII

PARIS, January 28, 1852.

DEAREST MOTHER:

Eight days ago I dispatched to you the chest
of books, and by this you must have duly received them. The list of books, to wit, the books
of which I wrote down the titles, has not been
sent back to me from Hamburg of late, and to-
day I must send you over a new list to boot. In
order to be sure that it shall not go astray again I
beg that you will have it copied at once. Campe

* The *coup d'état* thus foretold took place ; next year Napoleon
III placed upon his own head the imperial crown, and the down-
fall of the emperor took place fourteen years after the death of
the poet.

can use the new invoice of books, which Lotta will arrange, in order to pack among them a few books of his own on this occasion. I hope you are all well, and so far as I am concerned I find myself still in the same disgruntled frame of mind.

There is so much evil being done in the world just now that I am actually anxious and scared, and feel myself more uncomfortable than ever in this wretched skin of mine. Unhappily my wife also is in a bad temper, a direct result, it is true, of corporeal reasons. She suffers a good deal from headache. Winter creeps along in mournful fashion and I shall be glad when it is gone. My relations with the family are at this moment very objectionable, and that without my fault. We speak constantly of you, and I hope my dear Lotta you will soon send us a very gay letter. God keep you all and grant you health, which, as I notice unfortunately too late for myself, is the main point.

Here in Paris things are all in a snarl and we look forward to a mad to-morrow. Those who are well will shoot each other down, but the sickly have nothing to risk, and so you can be without anxiety on my account. I send hearty greeting

to my nieces, as well as to my nephew.   Farewell,
my dear, kind mother, and keep in affection
Your faithful son,
H. HEINE.

Heine wrought industriously on the complete
edition of his works in French and the clever
and often enthusiastic criticism of the works
which had appeared before was a new spur to
him to make the French public acquainted with
the product of his genius.

Les Œuvres complètes de Henri Heine, seven
volumes of which had appeared up to the time
of his death, won the most brilliant success and
placed him in the ranks of the first authors of
France.   Heine himself translated the prose
works in the most careful way, and all the finest
witty points are reflected therein after a
masterly fashion.   In the preface to the French
edition of his poems Heine does full justice to
the friends who undertook the difficult labor of
translating from the German.   Particularly was
he unable to think without emotion of his friend
Gérard de Nerval,* who during the evenings of

* This talented young French writer committed suicide, having
fallen into a melancholy.   He wrote a book on Germany.—TR.

March 1848 visited him every day in his isola-
tion near the *Barrière de la Santé* in order to
work with him on the translation of his peaceful
German fantasies, the while all about raged the
passions of politics and the monarchy went down
with a frightful noise. Deep in their idyllic and
æsthetic conversations, the two did not hear the
cry of the masses which was then sounding
through Paris—the masses howling their song,
Des Lampions! des lampions! the Marsellaise of
the February Revolution.

Heine also spoke with gratitude of his later
translators, while pointing out the temerity of
the attempt to render in the tongue of a
Romanic people the most profound and intimate
thoughts of a poetical work belonging to a
speech of the Germanic stock.

His poems were translated into French partly
in metrical form, partly in rhyme by René
Taillandier, Gérard de Nerval and Marelle; but
these translators allowed themselves, for the purpose of rhyming, many licenses, so that in the
metrical rendering the easy and poetic harmony
of the rhythm found in the original was lost.
Heine himself jested at the way and fashion

the tender, fragrant offspring of his muse had been treated, which in translation sounded about as sensible and prosaic as " bits of moonshine packed in straw " ! · It seemed to him while reading these translations as if somebody had taken him by the scalp lock, dragged him to the open market place, and called out, Hit him ! Hit him !

"Verily it seems to me as if I had looted the safe containing my literary worth in Germany and now were engaged at Paris in turning all my booty into money. Every time a German comes to see me a cold chill runs down my back, as if he were a secret agent of the German Parnassus who had obtained from the French Government my surrender and intended to lead me back thither where is howling and gnashing of teeth—I mean back to Germany. Yea, even after one thousand years have fled, I shall still be slandered, and all on account of these unfortunate translators ! "

CIV

PARIS, April 12, 1852.

DEAREST, KIND MOTHER :

To-day I only want to notify you that to-morrow I shall send off to your address by express

to Hamburg, a chest in which, besides the books
that I borrowed from the circulating library, there
is still another parcel which is meant for my
dear sister, Mrs. von Embden.

Among the books there is also the volume of my
tragedies which you lent me in Hamburg, as well
as two examples of my bronze medallion, one of
which likewise was lent me by you in Hamburg in
order that I might have more copies cast from it
here. One copy of the medallion, then, you are
to keep for yourself as before, and the other copy
of the medallion please send to Campe, to whom
I have promised it. The box must be opened
with the greatest care in order that the parcel for
Lotta which is therein shall not be damaged; for
it contains a silk gown, the very newest which
the season has brought forth, and exceedingly in
good taste, since my squanderer has chosen it.
You can rest assured that my wife obtains more
pleasure through this gift than if such a gown
had been presented to her. She is unfortunately
still affected with headaches very often. We
live in great unity, and she makes use of all her
charm in order to make me forget my sickly condition.

I am taken care of in the most extraordinary way, and yet she is my only bitterness—to use my old phrase. She asks to be heartily remembered to you all. I do the same and send compliments to the whole Goosemarket family! *

If I only knew of someone to carry off my Nanny from the Goosemarket! She must make a very nice dish by this time, particularly if stuffed with golden chestnuts and raisins. Nice behavior, simplicity in outward appearance, avoidance of everything that calls attention to her, absence of coquetry, love of truth and sweetness of temper are the traits which are of greatest use to young women.

Do write me whether the chest came duly to hand; you must have had to pay again an enormous freight, dear mother, and I am unable to arrange it otherwise, because the Cologne forwarders—a veritable band of robbers—blackmail each box. But these are the last books which I shall have sent me in this way, for the reason alone that the circulating library does not offer

* His brother-in-law had left his former home and moved into a dwelling on the corner of the Goosemarket and the Jungfernstieg.

me much I can use.   I shall make me better and cheaper channels.

Often if you do not get a letter from me for a long while, I can explain it thus: I have not always at hand a trusted friend to whom I can dictate German.   If I go into the country this summer you will often have to wait for a letter.

I love you with my whole soul.

Your faithful son,
H. HEINE.

CV

PARIS, June 12, 1852.

DEAR, KIND MOTHER AND DEAR SISTER:

Your letter, dear, kind mother, as well as Lotta's epistle, in which brother's arrival is announced, has filled me with the greatest pleasure. I can imagine the excitement into which this delightful surprise has plunged you.   I look forward with impatient expectation to the time when I shall embrace my dear Max after such a long separation.   All is the same with my health; it is as wearisome as repulsive to me if I have to be always threshing over again this subject *en détail.*   And I now never talk about my health

any more with those who come to see me. I
see my doctors little and am in need of nothing;
but am highly curious to hear what Max has to
say to me. You must assuredly write to me
the time at which I may expect him here, because owing to my nervous disease even pleasant
surprises are not good for me. My wife is warned
not to give me any surprise which she has not
exactly heralded twenty-four hours earlier.

I hope that mother is well and that you are
all sound and bright. Gustav will of course come
to Hamburg.

My wife seems pretty well; she complains
that she is not as pretty as before and for that
reason must wear more good clothes; I insist
upon the exact opposite—chiefly owing to the
cost of decorations! She has had her portrait
taken, but is not at all pleased with it; to obtain
peace and quiet I have to " cuss " that portrait.
But really she looks better *in natura* than *en
effigie.* But sometimes I'm fonder of the picture,
because it never scolds.*

And now farewell. Greetings to my nephew

* For verses written in exasperation at his wife's moods, see
vol. iii. 293. In better moods, pp. 121, 279, 285 and 286.—Tr.

and nieces and kisses to the latter. Dear Lotta,
I have written to Campe to have books sent
hither with Max. But let him understand as
soon as possible that this would cause too much
delay, and that I beg him, in case no other occasion
comes to hand, to send me the books without
delay by the railroad, post or the steamer.
Don't forget this.

How delighted I am to see my Max again! I
hardly believed that I should live long enough
for this joy.

Your faithful

H. HEINE.

CVI

PARIS, August 2, 1852.

MY DEAR, KIND MOTHER AND SISTER :

The departure of Max gave me great anguish
and I am as it were crushed by sorrow. It is a
great joy to see one another again after so long
a separation, but one has to pay dearly for it
with the anguish of separation. My wife is in
the same mood and Calypso could not have been
more sorrowful at the departure of Ulysses than
my squanderer has been at the departure of Max.
The latter struck a bad streak here, since he came

bang into the great hot term, and I, whom it exhausted frightfully, could not spare him a single well hour. I suffered much from the heat, but now that the weather is better I am on the mend. Max will give you news by word of mouth concerning everything that relates to me, and for some time I shall need to write you little ; that suits me well, since at the moment I am very much occupied.

We have talked about you constantly in all trustiness and tenderness. We have been much amused at Ludwig's remark about the miraculous stigmata of our martyr. We love him at bottom quite unusually ; he has such a kind heart. I send kisses to my niece Anna, and to my own Lena, who is a very nice girl. Write to me as soon as Max arrives.

Is Carl in Hamburg? Max will tell you how much trouble and care it takes in Paris to arrange one's self comfortably if one is sickly, how my squanderer attends to my nursing, and that nothing is lacking or forgotten which can be procured for money. There is no saving; on the contrary ; but the main point—rest—is very difficult to procure in this place. And yet Paris affords me greater advantages than other places, where much more vexatious torments would be sure to await me.   My wife asks to be heartily remembered, and there are few fat women who are as sweet and lovable in this heat as she.

I embrace you both, and am

Your faithful

H. HEINE.

CVII

PARIS, September 30, 1852.

DEAREST MOTHER:

I delayed writing because beforehand I wanted to await a letter from Max at Hamburg; but it appears 'that he has left you without having written me before he went, according to our compact, which is a great and unpardonable piece of negligence concerning which I shall say nothing, because otherwise I might express myself too bitterly.   I, who by reason of my sickness do not have my arms free and often sit in a great whirl of work, I nevertheless do not neglect the least detail, and Max, who is occupied with care of himself alone, acts frivolously, as a poet would scarcely have a right to do.

I hope that both of you are feeling well, and

from you, mother, I hope soon to see letters. I write you to-day chiefly in order to notify you that I am sending to your address, and that per steamer from Havre, a chest of books which unfortunately I can prepay only as far as Havre; so I must again beg that you will lay out a goodly sum for me, and beg you to tell me exactly how much it cost. In the box is a lot of books which Lotta's manager of the circulating library Mr. Jovien sent me hither without being requested. I beg you to see that they go back with much thanks (since one should be thankful for any and every courtesy), but accompanied by the prayer that he should never again send me books hither which I have not ordered in accordance with my own selection, since he could not know that I cared to read a single one of them; and so pay freight expenses to no purpose. Then you will find in the box another lot of books, all of which have on their title pages the stamp of Bernhardt's circulating library and moreover have rose-colored tickets for numbers on the back, while the books from Jovien carry a green number-ticket on the back. These books from the Bernhardt circulating library were sent me by Campe. I beg Lotta to take exact care that the books be not mixed together.

Perhaps you have learned from Max how I fell into confusion through Gustav's unsuitable conversation with Campe. Since Gustav is my brother and at the worst committed a stupidity through too much zeal, certainly I shall be the last to growl at him for so doing. Let him gossip about me as much as he chooses, and even about my wife, as Max says; let him follow his natural character as he will, since I have known him to possess always that character and for forty years have ever forgiven him; he shall always be to me the beloved brother whose finer traits I value all the more. And it is not to be denied that he has good qualities. I know him through and through and understand exactly the genealogy of his faults. He is not the first of his sort. The censorship does not permit me to say more.

And now, dear Lotta, how is it with you? How is your youthful brood? the two big pullets and the boy? I talk about you with my wife every day; she asks to be heartily remembered. I am not so badly off in health. At the opening of the season I had a rough time, but now I am

feeling very well. I am well cared for and work
but little. In no event shall I do work for
nothing. Everything is quiet here, and as Gustav is not present, we live in peace and harmony.
Is Carl still in Hamburg? Let me know. Anyhow, write to me soon.

Here is the page ended, and I embrace you both.

Your faithful

H. HEINE.

CVIII

PARIS, December 29, 1852.

DEAREST, KIND MOTHER, MY DEAR, KIND
SISTER, AND EVERYTHING ELSE THAT BUMPS
AND BOUNCES ABOUT YOU:

I have received with pleasure the letter which
speaks of mother's birthday festival, and greatly
was I delighted thereat. To-day I send congratulation for the new year, which announces itself
pretty kindly for me. I cherish the hope that
the new year will be better than the old. I
hardly need to tell you now that I wish you
everything that is nice and good. May Heaven
keep you in health, harmony and sweetness of
mood! My wife also asks me to give her con-

gratulations, and is just in the act of decorating the windows with new white curtains in order to receive the new year in a courteous fashion. Her mood is extremely charming, and this year she makes fewer New Year presents—which verily is a step in advance! She sends friendly greeting to my nephew Ludwig and I too send regards to Ludwig as well as to my brother-in-law Moritz. I send hearty greeting also to Anna and Lena and shall find occasion before the end of next month to let them know that they have in Paris an uncle who loves them greatly.

I kiss my darling mother all over her face, and both her dear hands too. My wife says that dear mother must certainly have looked very well in the new cap.

And now farewell. Write to me much, and keep in affection

Your faithful

H. HEINE.

CIX

PARIS, March 18, 1853.

DEAREST, KIND MOTHER:

It is not my fault if I do not write to you oftener, for my German secretary is sick nowadays and can rarely come to see me. That is why I delayed sending an answer at once to your last letter. You complain because I do not write with my own hand. Don't do that any more, otherwise I shall write you with my own hand, but that effort will cost me every time a headache for three days. If I strain my eyes in the slightest degree I get my old headaches back again, and you know what that means. When I write, that is, when I use my own hand, it has always to be done with a pencil, and the result is very illegible; but illegibility does not do at all for letters, and besides, I should confine myself to the most necessary information alone. At this moment I have much to do and can spare myself but little. As long as a man is alive he must carry on his work, and in my isolated condition nobody can help me.

My wife is in good health and at this moment is very happy because I have bought for a considerable sum a lot of linen for the household. Linen gives her more pleasure than pretty clothes, and that is very praiseworthy. We live in great unity, that is, I yield in all things. We are ever talking of you both—and now farewell.

I greet you heartily, my dear Lotta, and kiss you and your children. In your next letter, dear Lotta, do write me down the number on the Goosemarket in case I should have to send anyone to your address.

Latterly Dr. Wille visited me; he lives now in Zurich. It is a great question whether Therese will visit me if she comes to Paris. I doubt it much, because in every possible way they will try to prevent it.

I kiss you both.

Your faithful

H. HEINE.

CX

PARIS, May 7, 1853.

DEAREST MOTHER:

About eight days ago I received a letter from our Lotta, but as not a line from you was within, the assurance of sister that you are in good health is not so very satisfactory, and I beg you to send me a few words very soon. I am in my ordinary state and my wife too is at the present moment well. She has been very wretched, as in general she is not entirely strong and perhaps in later years will have to bear a good deal of pain, or else, since she has no talent for a quiet life of sickliness, she will not reach any great age.   At the present time we find ourselves in such a tender harmony of spirit that the angels might well envy us; and this creature, kind to the depths of her soul, in whose heart not one drop is false, and who does not so much as conceive the wickedness of the world—verily she sweetens for me my sufferings!

An article by me in a French review has had frightful success,* but to my greatest bitterness I must learn that this fine work has been published in Berlin by a wretched German bookseller in a wretched German translation, and that not at all in a periodical, which would have been all the same to me, but as a separate pamphlet, at the appearance of which Campe has again shown the most violent excitement.   Through this publication goes to pieces a scheme to publish the work in question this very year, for which I have still to write a continuation, bound up with other articles.   Thus is my property stolen away from under my own nose by my be-

* *Les Dieux en Exil* in the *Revue des Deux Mondes.*

loved fellow-countrymen and great damages
done me for the sake of a little profit. Nevertheless I shall not begin any row, as Campe
would like me to. I am certain that the vagabond who made this translation is a literary
sectarian from the school of a Salomon or a Klei;
this I have smelt out from various turns of speech,
but still more from fragments in the newspapers,
which he has had printed in his patchwork
besides, and in which he gives all sorts of garbled
news of my health and would even like to give
himself the appearance of a kind-hearted friend!

My life is made cursedly hard for me and in
good sooth our Lord and Savior must be a god
in order that he could pardon in such Pharisees
their passion for persecution!

Monsieur Wihl had the kindness to chuck himself out of the house, and a still dirtier, still viler
and much more dangerous vagabond, the litterateur W., is never, thank God, to cross my threshold again. There is a mob of fellows of this
kidney in Paris who run about and gossip, or
even correspond, and whom, thank God, I do
not see.

Oh dear, if I could only talk myself out with

Lotta for an hour or two! I greet all heartily.
Farewell, keep in love

Your faithful

H. HEINE.

CXI

PARIS, June 21, 1853.

DEAREST, KIND MOTHER:

I don't know which of us owes an answer to
the other, but I have nothing to report except
that I am in good health, as good at least as
is possible in my long and wearisome illness.
My wife was well until yesterday evening, when
she complained a little ; but I hope that it means
nothing.   I always lose my head at once as soon
as anything is amiss with my dear wife.   Men
are big fools!   But the biggest fools are those
men who do not love their wives, because they
have to make the same expenditure for them and
for the same money might obtain for themselves
a bit of tenderness.

I send greetings to my dear Lotta and the
children.   I beg you to particularly kiss my dear
niece Anna.   Therese has visited me here, but in
company with Carl, who was sent to act as sen-

tinel, so that I should say nothing she ought not
to hear!

I am always thinking of you, dear mother, and
love you unutterably.

I work a great deal, which of course attacks my
strength, but at the same time does good by
diverting my thoughts.

I embrace you tenderly and pray to God who
is kind that he keep you well and gladsome.

Your faithful son,

H. HEINE.

CXII

PARIS, July 16, 1853.

DEAREST SISTER:

Pardon me for not answering your letter at
once ; I had no one at hand to whom I could dictate German. In answer to the question contained in the paper forwarded to me, regarding
my biography, I shall only say a few words.

You know what my baptismal and surname are,
as well as the names of our parents, so that you
can fill up this rubric. The names of my wife are
Mathilde Creszenzia Heine; I like best to call
her Mathilde, because the name Creszenzia, which

is also that of her mother, has always given me a pain in the throat. As to the date of my birth I have to say that according to my notice of baptism I was born the thirteenth of December, 1799, and that at Düsseldorf on the Rhine, as must likewise be known to you. Since all our family papers were destroyed at Hamburg in the conflagration, and in the register at Düsseldorf the date of my birth could not have been properly entered—for reasons which I do not care to mention—the above date alone is authentic—at any rate more authentic than the recollections of my mother, whose aging memory is not capable of replacing any papers which are lost.

As to the schools in which I was polished off, they too are known to you; they begin with the Franciscan monastery at Düsseldorf; later I passed two years in the Protestant Institute of Vahrenkamp, afterward I attended all the classes at the lyceum, which is now called the gymnasium. The teachers of the Franciscan monastery, as well as those of the lyceum, will be recalled by mother, and I think there is no need of mentioning them here. At the Universities of Bonn, Göttingen and Berlin, where later I passed some years, I enjoyed tuition from very celebrated persons, but it is too tedious for me to reel off the list of their names. Now as regards the books, in this particular I will refer to Campe, who knows the facts better than I do myself, and so he can fill up the rubric in question. For the rest, I think there is nothing more to mention and what has already been stated bores me quite enough.

When you see Mr. Campe beg him in my name to give the list of books which I drew up from the Lacisz catalogue and in accordance with which he was to send me an invoice which has never come to hand. Do send me this list at once in order that I may strike out the books which I no longer need and send you a new list, so that I can get the books forwarded whose dispatch Campe has delayed so long, so unwarrantably long! I would write to him direct if I did not have also to answer his last letter and if at this moment I did not lack the spirit. For in his last letter he has again blamed me, as if it were I who laid obstacles in his way and who broke up our good relations by demanding too much money from him. Heaven knows that I make no demands on him for anything which I do not believe myself to have earned twice over. For the rest my brothers have done their part in bringing on that confusion which exists between Campe and me and is now no longer to be altered.

For the rest Max is far more to blame than Gustav, since in his egotism he did not even take the trouble to read carefully the letters in which I gave him the strictest instructions with regard to Campe. He might have made him concessions, if not with regard to the sum of money, still with respect to other interests which have money value for Campe—and the affair would have been quite simple. Instead of that the fool preaches to me to rely blindly on Campe's friendship, and tries to persuade me there is no need for me to make such a point of money—and I ought to permit my fleece to be sheared now as before. So I have not written to him since he reached Russia, because when I do write something bitter might slip out, and on such occasions silence is the best.

I write you under the address of my dear mother so that the greetings that I shall send her herewith may reach her a few hours earlier. Right heartily do I kiss dear, kind mother; and

Mathilde too, who has been very sick but is restored again, asks to forward you the tenderest
caresses. I am merely so-so; only this powerful heat has regaled me with permanent headache.

My most friendly greetings to your husband
and your children as well.

Jolly and loving,

Your faithful

H. HEINE.

CXIII

PARIS, August 18, 1853.

DEAREST, KIND MOTHER:

With delight I have seen from your last letter that you are in good health. To be sure I
have no greater warrant than your own letter,
and many a time do I worry greatly on your
account. But you know our agreement. Do
not complain because I rarely write, for you
know that I do not have anyone at each moment at my command in order to dictate German.

My wife is very well, but at the present moment
she is not in my possession, for owing to family
matters she has gone for two days to her home
and will not come back till this evening.

I send hearty greetings to my dear Lotta and her children. I thank Lotta for her last letter and will send her back presently a list of books. I have just had another letter from Campe, though I had not answered his last epistle ; once more he questions my wish to be of service in all kinds of ways, and I can see how he is choking with exasperation because I will not permit myself to be exploited by him without a proviso. He announced that he is again issuing a new edition of the " Buch der Lieder."* Not a line of manuscript does he get from me for nothing, and so I let everything lie in my portfolio.

Everything is quiet here and the fear of a war is gone. Nevertheless I believe that war will inevitably break out next year, because the relations and the interests are too much mixed up. A lucifer match can set the world in flames just now, and the firemen† who are in command show more anxiety than sense.

And now farewell, dear mother, and be assured that I think of you day and night. Our

---

* Bought at one time by Campe for fifty louis d'or.

† 1853–56. The Eastern question and the war of the Crimea which sprang from it.

whole relationship, to be sure, only consists in the fact that you are my old discursive mother, but at the same time you are such a perfectly square woman and such a dear old Mausel that I can never get enough of you, and with the highest respect love you unspeakably.

Your obedient son,

H. HEINE.

CXIV

PARIS, December 7, 1853.

DEAR, KIND MOTHER:

I am not very well acquainted with the accursed Russian calendar and know not whether Counselor of State Kiseleff is to make his visit this week or the next. To-day I write to congratulate you on your birthday and I think once more with laughter of little Paul's congratulations made last year with a pot of flowers.*

May Heaven, dear mother, grant you a vast deal of happiness and keep you as always lively and in good health. Cold has already arrived here

---

* This little grandson of Heine's mother brought her a pot of hyacinths and when the grandmother, thanking him, reached forward to take it, the child burst into tears and would not give it up.

and I think with terror how the coming winter may be able to assault you in your little dove-cote. Would that I could get to you in order to stop up every crevice where a draft could get through! We talk of you constantly and my wife says that it seems to her as if she had left you but yesterday—but to my mind it is as if I were ever by your side.

With respect to my health, I am getting on as usual, and verily I know not what I could add to this answer of Canonicus Karthümel. I am still suffering from cramps, but these do not, as they did with my father of blessed memory, affect the stomach. I hope that you all live in gayety and unity. I am very quiet indeed and agree that five is an even number. Nothing has turned out luckily for me in this world, but still I might have had a worse fate. That is the way that half-whipped dogs comfort themselves.

I hope to write you again in this year, and as you know that I still have no German secretary at command you will gladly pardon me if my congratulations for the year do not reach you at the proper time.

Everything here is quiet and all Paris is occu-

pied with building. Everything is torn down,
built up afresh ; and one scarcely knows any more
where the old corners are to be found. I am
highly pleased with my wife and she is the truest
soul anyone could imagine. Of course when all is
said, I believe there is only a solitary person
upon whom a man can entirely rely, and that person is his mother. Here a person is entirely
sure ; whoever doubts that, for him no course is
more to be recommended than that he should
leave this world as soon as possible.

And now, dear mother, farewell. I greet my
dear Lotta and her dear children from my heart
and embrace you all with the most profound love.

Your faithful son,

H. HEINE.

Heine's health had become decidedly worse
again because of a heavy cold. Inflammation of
the neck, accompanied by violent cramps of
throat and breast, made breathing difficult, and
moreover a swelling had come out on his back
which made lying down torture. It was necessary to submit to a painful operation and the poet
thought he was near his end. After the opera-

tion the condition of the sick man improved and hardly had a lessening of his torments set in when he commenced to work unweariedly.

Soon afterward, in the spring of 1854, my sister * went to Paris in order to visit her uncle, and with reference to this meeting wrote that she scarcely could recognize him when she saw that figure of suffering, and found him so changed that tears prevented her from speaking. Paralysis of his eyelids prevented him from observing her sorrow.

"'Step nearer, dear child,' he said in a weak voice 'in order that I may see you ; here, close to me !'" And with one hand he raised his eyelid in order to see whether she looked like her mother.

"I had to take a seat on the bed, and the first questions he asked were about the dear ones at home.

"'Alas! I shall never see my beloved mother again, and my dear Lotta—will she not come soon?' he cried in a tone of sorrow."

My sister reported further :

* Marie, Princess della Rocca, published in 1881 " Reminiscences regarding Heinrich Heine " through Hoffmann & Campe, Hamburg ; and in 1882, " Sketches relating to Heinrich Heine," through A. Hartleben, Leipsic.

"The evening before my departure I sat by his side. He had told me of his youthful years and combats with men and I was silently listening to his recollections. Wearied out, he lay there almost lifeless; the sick room was badly lighted; a lamp was burning dimly behind a screen and one heard the monotonous ticking of a clock. I did not dare disturb his rest and sat motionless on my chair. Suddenly he tried to change his position, a thing the doctor had earnestly warned him not to do, since it ought to be done only with the assistance of the nurse. He was seized with cramps and moaned and groaned in the most frightful manner.

"The scene was a new one to me; I thought it was the death struggle when I saw him wrestling for breath, and from the depths of my soul I prayed to God to loose him from these torturing pains. Pauline, his faithful caretaker, sought to quiet him, and assured me that it was a passing pain and that she had often seen him in this condition. Nothing could keep me longer in the chamber; I ran sobbing away and only saw him again for a few moments in order to say farewell. It was for eternity! . . ."

Besides his illness Heine was saddened by the disagreeable state of things with his old friend Julius Campe, whose hardness as to money payments gave him much trouble and bitterness. Up to that time Campe had been accustomed to buy Heine's manuscripts cheap and felt himself deeply wounded because the poet, crowned by fame, placed higher demands for payment on his writings. Heine's pecuniary condition had entirely altered since the publication of his works in French, which were paid for in a brilliant fashion, and as the former dependence of a needy man on his German publisher had vanished, he was able to await the acceptance of his demands in the greatest quiet.

Heine was now earning a good deal of money, paid off all his former debts, and as early as the close of 1851 used his first surplus to pay back to his brother Gustav everything which he had borrowed from him.

It gave him great pleasure to be unburdened of his old money troubles; this permitted him to give his mother, sister and nieces presents now and then, and to meet the often far-reaching desires of Mathilde.

CXV

PARIS, June 26, 1854.

DEAR, KIND LOTTA:

My wife has enjoyed the pleasure of hunting up a gown for you cut according to the latest fashion and two gowns for my nieces— altogether *uni*, I assure you—and I send them to you by rail in a special box which is addressed to your husband. I send you to-day, it is true, a manuscript to Campe at the same time; but I did not want to pack the gowns in his box, because he is married and women grudge each other everything!

The gown *gris de perle* I have assigned to Nanny and the blue one to Lena, whom you expect back in Hamburg, as you told me. I counsel you not to send the gown across the sea even if you have the chance, because the salt air will hurt the color. But if the little blonde stays away too long you are authorized, if you wish, to give the blue gown also to the brunette who stayed at home, and hereby I tell you in advance that this arrangement also will suit me.

I have bought nothing for mother, because she

would not let anybody make her a pompous gown in any case and would only screech. I therefore beg you to buy a marvel of a cap for her in Hamburg and tell her that it was packed in your box; buy as fine a one as possible and tell me how much you have paid out for it. I have carefully noted the name which you have mentioned and shall write you on the matter; I shall not forget.

Unhappily I am not getting on well this summer. Day and night I suffer from cramps and do not get away from bed. My wife conducts herself admirably, and amused herself ten times more with buying the dresses than if they had been for her own use. But she shall have her reward for it. I cannot do without her in my sufferings, and am horrified by the thought that I must leave her!

Farewell, dear sister. Greet for me heartily Nanny and Ludwig, as well as your husband.

Your faithful brother,

H. HEINE.

P. S.—You can have no conception how much I have had to bear from the Jesuit,* and how he

* Julius Campe, his publisher.

has done everything possible to torture me. But we are the best of friends. Do you recall a certain " Red Aaron " ?

CXVI

PARIS, August 31, 1854.

DEAR, KIND MOTHER:

I have a great piece of news to impart to you to-day. It is this: I have entirely given up my old abode in Paris and now live near the Bar- rière of Paris in a house which I occupy alone and to which belongs quite a big garden with quite big trees, and where I can enjoy this lovely season in the most delightful way. I have made the greatest sacrifices of money in order to make this revolution, and verily do not regret it, since my health will be extraordinarily furthered thereby. My present system is to do everything for my health and nothing for other people, not even for the squanderer, to whom in any case I could not bequeath enough. My address is *aux Batignolles, grand rue No.* 51, *à Paris.*

You have no conception, dear mother, how greatly the fine air and sunshine which I did not have in my old abode does me good. Yester-

day I sat in better health than ever under the
trees of my own garden and ate the fine plums
which fell overripe into my mug. I thought of
you all and made the resolve to write to you
to-day, although I am still in the greatest confusion. My wife (who always calls herself, when
she speaks of herself, *meine Frau* in German, a
thing that comes out very comically, like a parrot)
asks to be heartily remembered. She tells me
just now to say : " *Dis à ma mère que ' meine
Frau' est très occupée, et que ' meine Frau' l'em-
brasse mille fois.*"

I send hearty greetings to my Lotta, as well as
to the young ladies and Ludwig.

I have obtained the best news of X. from a
lady who is very truthful. He is said to be a
very good fellow, very companionable, and also
to possess elsewhere a little property, that is not
confiscated like his landed estate at home, which
will probably be handed back to him if he will
crawl to kiss the cross politically. As he now
has a cross in his house, he will probably soon
come to a peace with such thoughts, and properly duck his head.

I have left entirely to Campe the correcting of

the proofs for two volumes, and would rather **be**
immortal a few years less than strain my eyes **too**
much.

Keep in your love

Your faithful

H. HEINE.

CXVII

PARIS, November 6, 1854.

DEAR NANNY :

I wanted to write to you long ago, but never
reached the point because there was such a
banging and bouncing round my ears ! To-day
also I am not in condition to say an intelligible
word to you. Your sweet letter amused me
greatly, and we laughed heartily at your drawing.
My wife loves you very much and sends hearty
greetings to you, as well as to your father, your
brother, Lena and of course your mother.

Herewith I send you an autograph, for which
your father will count you out twelve yellow
louis d'or. Buy with it something that pleases
you; in that way you make it unnecessary for
me to buy it, pack it and forward it, and so do
me a service for which I thank you.

Notify me also of the receipt of this letter. As soon as I shall be at all in a pleasant mood I will write you further.

Meantime farewell, and be ever lovingly devoted.

Your faithful uncle,
HENRY HEINE.

CXVIII

PARIS, November 7, 1854.

DEAREST, GOOD MOTHER:

I did not want to write to you before I could certainly notify you that I had moved; but the moving was delayed from day to day by all kinds of events and it was not till yesterday that I arrived safely in my new house. It was a journey of about two hours, but one in which I was favored by the best of weather. As you can imagine I find myself in the greatest disorder; have a thousand matters on every side, and to-day must limit myself to merely imparting to you my new address. It reads as follows: *aux Champs Elysées, 3 avenue Matignon, Paris.*

Just think: till this moment I have not yet received a copy of my book from Campe. The

devil would learn wisdom from the poison mixing
the latter is working at. I hope to get entirely
at rest in a few weeks. I greet my dear sister
and her children. I embrace you all heartily.

Your faithful son,

H. HEINE.

Heine had forsaken the house in Batignolles,
which was too damp, and had moved into the
Champs Elysées. The new abode was admirably placed and entirely in accord with Heine's
wishes; it was on the third floor, without noises
overhead, roomy, bright and airy. It was provided with a balcony on to which he had himself carried on sunny, windless days, in order to
watch the promenaders and equipages with their
well dressed fares, who hurried toward the Arc
de Triomphe in order to push on to the Bois de
Boulogne. This diversion often gave the poet
pleasure and caused him to grow so fond of his
new home that he stayed there to his end.

Besides the literary and artistic magnates of
France who visited Heine, it had become the
fashion for German authors to make a pilgrimage
to him as the Mohammedans journey to Mecca.

After their return home all kinds of imaginary things and witty speeches were often related in feuilletons and articles, in order to show the public the stamp of genuineness on their Paris visit.

In the winter of 1855 Heine's condition grew worse and brought on a return of his sufferings of the year before; this time he once more overcame the passing peril, and after a short period of convalescence devoted himself again to his labor.

CXIX

PARIS, March 20, 1855.

DEAREST SISTER :

I am suffering in an extraordinary way at this moment from cramps in the throat, and for that reason am in no condition to write much to you to-day. A few days ago I dispatched a box to you on the Goosemarket, but without a street number, by the *Messageries Royales ;* it is to be hoped that the railway or postal officials in your town know the address of Moritz; if not, you must send to the station in order to get news of the arrival of the box. There is a hat in it for

you, and in order to make use of the occasion I
sent along a hat for Nanny and one for Lena
also. Both of the last are quite simple, and the
light blue hat is for the blonde and the rose-
colored hat for the brunette. I hope that yours,
likewise bluish and somewhat more serious, will
be very becoming to you, and that by its means
I shall win your patronage for the future also.
Unfortunately I was able to prepay the box only
to Brussels and you will have to pay a heathenish
freight for it.

My wife sends you friendly and hearty greetings. It has given her great pleasure to undertake the ordering of the hats and one can rely
upon her good taste. I kiss you all; greet my
nephew heartily and pray greet your husband
likewise for me.

My French books give me a frightful lot of
bang and bounce. In a fortnight the "Lutetia" *
will be out in French. I have no news concerning Carl and I beg you to tell me how he is and
where. Do keep my dear, old mother nice and

* For "Lutetia, or Reports on Politics, Art and Popular Life,'
see vol. ix. p. 205, and vol. x. It appeared in German in 1832.
—Tr,

warm. She is a very pride and joy! God keep
you all!

Your faithful brother,

H. HEINE.

On its appearance in 1855 the "Lutetia"
created a great sensation, and in the preface to this
edition Heine, in his well known humorous way
of writing, laid the lash on Socialism, at that time
already rising with boldness. He said :

"Only with terror and shuddering do I think
upon that epoch in which these darksome icono-
clasts shall win their way to sovereignty. With
their horny hands they will pitilessly break to
pieces all the marble statues of beauty which are
dear to my heart. They will tear into bits all
those fantastic toys and tinsel of art which the poet
so loves. They will fell my groves of laurel in
order to plant potatoes there. The lilies which
neither spun nor yet labored and still were as
magnificently clothed as was King Solomon in all
his glory, these shall be torn up from the garden
of society in case they perchance refuse to take
a spindle in their hands. The roses, lazy
brides of the nightingales, will be overtaken by

the same fate. The nightingales, those useless singers, will be driven off and alas! my 'Book of Songs' will serve the peddler of spices as material from which to twist cornucopias and into these he will pour coffee or snuff for the old beldames of the future. Alas, I see all this in advance, and an. inexpressible sadness creeps over me when I think of the destruction which a victorious proletariat threatens to bring upon my verses, which will sink into the grave along with the entire ancient, romantic world!"

And further: "Dante says the devil is a logician! A horrible syllogism has me in its embrace, and if I am not able to refute the statement 'that all men have a right to eat,' I am compelled to surrender and submit myself to all the consequences thereof.* While I think of that I run the risk of losing my mind; I see all the godlike powers of truth dancing triumphantly about me and at last my soul seizes on a high-hearted despair and I cry out: 'Long ago it was judged and sentenced—this old society! Let that happen to it which is right!'"

* For verses on the conflict between those who have and those who lack, see "Die Wanderratten," vol. iii. p. 228.—TR,

My mother had a great longing to see her brother once more, and, disquieted by the acute form which his sufferings had assumed, she wrote that she wished to come to Paris to nurse him herself as soon as her household duties would permit.

CXX

PARIS, August 10, 1855.

DEAREST MOTHER :

Since your last letter I think of nothing else save the happy seeing of my dear sister once more. Everything is already arranged, so that on her arrival at our house my dear Lotta shall find a livable room where Lotta and one of my nieces (for I should be greatly delighted if she brought Anna or Lena with her) will find themselves comfortable. Indeed it would be an unending pleasure for me if Lotta brought with her likewise one of the dear children, Nanny or Lena, never mind which, for both are equally dear to me and only age decides the precedence. We live here with room to our elbows, and all our friends who come to see us admire the fine view and the good air which we enjoy, so that we find ourselves in the most brilliant center of

Paris and yet seem to be in the country. Last week Laube and his wife from Vienna were in town and often came to see us; Friedland and his wife from Prague also. This man, as I once reported to you, has already repaid me a portion of the damages into which I stumbled through him, and as I have bills of exchange and he is very wealthy, I shall lose nothing in the end.

Dr. L. also, who brought me a letter of introduction from Lotta, visited me eight days ago. He seems to be an extremely charming man, has a fine exterior, talks by no means like a fool, and promised me to visit me soon again. He will stay here five weeks more and so I told him that he would see Lotta here within that time.

My wife is well and is very gay. I am still suffering from my old trouble, 'the cramps, which to be sure are not very painful, but hinder me in every enjoyment of life, and particularly in working.

I am still diplomatizing with Campe, and even if he should stand on his head I shall not allow myself any longer to be "shaved across the spoon" by him. He must be secretly much en-

raged with me and of course is playing me all
kinds of tricks behind my back. But I am tacking, and at last I shall reach what I wish. He
will be furious when he learns that Lotta and
Gustav are coming to Paris. Schiff seems to be
his man of all work, and Lotta should look out
for herself.

My wife greets and kisses you all heartily and
my Insignificance does the same. I embrace you
tenderly, my kind, excellent mother, and with
profoundest love remain,

Your faithful son,

H. HEINE.

CXXI

PARIS, October 24, 1855.

DEAR, KIND MOTHER:

I have no German secretary now and can write
you but little with my own hand—hence my delay. Moreover I expect the family every day
and they must surely be on the road by this.
Lotta's bed is already made. I wrote lately to
Gustav and congratulated him on his new creation. He is the one to continue our line; I have
brought everything to naught. I have also

thanked Gustav for the honor done me by calling his boy after me. If he is still in Hamburg I beg him warmly to make peace with Campe; this quarrel has caused me great vexation and damage. Perhaps Lotta can work as a peacemaker by asking in person of Campe for any messages to Paris. Let Campe send me through her the third part of Meissner's novel.

Nanny will not lose much if she does not come here this year, as Lotta writes—and for many reasons. But I hope that conjunctions will present themselves in spring which will guarantee a more pleasurable journey hither. Society is beginning to move about now and the child would not be prepared for that during a short stay. Apropos—if Lotta is still in Hamburg and by chance should have my book,* "Shakespeare's Maidens and Women," I beg that she may bring it with her; not to be had here any more.

I kiss you, precious mother.

Your faithful son,

H. HEINE.

* See vol. iv. of the Bibliothek Ausgabe.—TR.

CXXII

Monsieur,
> *Mr. Hermann Heine,**
>> *à Hambourg.*

PARIS, November 19, 1855.

DEAREST HERMANN:

I have just learned through Lotta what a loss
you suffered lately, and although I am very ill
and almost blind, still I want to condole with
you under my own hand. Deeply has the sorrowful news grieved me! My dear uncle Henry
was an excellent, good man, sweet and kindly to
the verge of weakness, and for that reason all the
more lovable. He was courteous, decorous, possessed of good manners; no coarse word and
still less a wounding speech ever came from his
lips. He never told a lie, and even as with
subtle meanness, so with rude and insulting hate-
fulness, both were entirely foreign to his heart.

---

* The original belongs to Dr. H. Oswalt in Frankfort on the
Main, nephew of [the other] Henry Heine.

Henry Heine, born 1774, died 1855, married Henriette Embden, born 1787, died 1868, and left two children :

Hermann, born 1816, died 1870.

Emilie, married to S. Oswalt in Frankfort, born 1818, died
1892.

But especially one had to praise this in him: he was an utterly honest man!

An utterly honest man he was, my poor, blessed uncle, and I hear with pleasure, dear Hermann, that you are like him in this particular. Such fine traits as his are unfortunately becoming very rare; falseness and lies are in the majority, and where evil has been sowed there shall people reap bad luck and ruin! The tears of the insulted clamor to God (whose hand lies also very heavy upon me—whether as a penal judgment or a discipline I do not know). I suffer greatly, but support my wretchedness with submission to the unfathomable will of God.

I cannot see any longer the letters I am writing and hasten to greet you in the most brotherly way.

Your faithful cousin
H. HEINE.

Before the arrival of the preceding letters my mother had reached Paris in company with her brother Gustav. She sent me the following with regard to the meeting with her brother Heinrich:

"Mathilde stood on the threshold, embraced me, and said that before I entered the house my brother had called her and remarked: 'I feel that Lotta is coming; there is no need of preparing for her, bring her at once to me; I shall not lose a minute in seeing her!' When I stepped up to his bed he clasped me long in his arms with the cry: 'My darling Lotta!' without uttering a word, then leaned his head on my shoulder and reached out his hand to his brother.

"His delight at seeing me cannot be described, and I was not permitted to leave his bedside until late at night except for dinner. From the previous reports which I had heard concerning the illness of my brother I feared that the first sight of his sufferings would have shaken me profoundly, but when I saw merely the head, which smiled upon me with its wonderful illumined beauty, I was able to give myself up to the first pleasure of seeing him once more.

"Yet near afternoon when the nurse carried my brother in her arms to an invalid's chair in order to make up the bed, and I saw the body all shrunk together, from which his legs hung down without signs of life, I had to gather all my

powers of self-control in order to support in
quiet that horrible sight.

"My bed was arranged close to the sick
chamber and during the very first night long
continued cramps of chest and head made their
appearance; they worried me greatly. Almost
every night such attacks repeated themselves
and when I then hastened to his bedside, at
once the laying of my hand on the sick man's
brow seemed to bring him relief. My brother
often said that I possessed strange magnetic
powers which he felt at once no matter how
gently I crept into the room.

"At moments when he was free from pain the
recollections of former years in the parental
house or concerning relatives were able to raise
a laugh in him again, and if Mathilde was
present she would laugh aloud and only then
ask, since she did not understand German, what
it was we were laughing at so hard

"Mathilde lived with me in the best reciprocal
understanding; not so with Gustav, who spoke
no French and could not come to an understanding with her; this produced a tension on both
sides. Besides, Gustav thought the marriage of

his brother for love a great mishap; according to his opinion it was the source of his failures and sufferings. Mathilde, who was accustomed to a certain petting, counted Gustav's reserve for discourtesy, and while translating I was often at my wit's end how to preserve a superficial friendship by means of little improvisations. After a drive Gustav would perhaps give the cabby too small a tip. The latter, thrusting it into his pocket, would murmur *ladre* (thief!). Mathilde would laugh loudly and at Gustav's inquiry why she laughed so immoderately I would reply : 'It's nothing ; he was merely thanking you for the tip you gave him!'

" Scenes of this kind repeated themselves several times, and when Gustav returned to Vienna, leaving me behind in Paris, I was glad that no serious quarrel had arisen between them. Mathilde's easily roused temper often occasioned outbursts of wrath over matters of no importance and my brother had to suffer in especial from her jealous temperament. He bore this with stoical quiet and knew how to soothe it quickly with a few jocose remarks.

" The entire left side of my brother was paralyzed, the left eye blinded, arm and hand powerless. Only the right side of his body preserved the power of nerve action, so that it was still possible for him to write with the right hand. Often did he place that hand in mine and assure me that my presence was a great comfort ; I could scarcely conceive, he said, what a pleasure he found in being able to chat so confidentially ; and when the subject of our recoilections of happy childhood was exhausted I was made to tell everything about mother and my children. A few months before, he said, when his secretary of many years' standing, Richard Reinhold, left him, he had begun to feel very much the solitude of the sick chamber ; daily visitors had exhausted rather than pleased him, and the writers engaged on trial through advertisements in the papers had afforded him no satisfactory substitute. Latterly, an inspiriting person of uncommon gifts had come to see him, a German woman, a lively offspring of Swabia, who combined in herself French wit with German heartiness. She read aloud to him in a melodious voice and was so well acquainted with French that he was able to leave to her the correction of proofs for his works. She had been slightly under the weather, but would soon come again, and he was curious to learn what kind of impression she would make on me.*

" Mouche, as my brother called her because of her seal, on which a fly was engraved, was in fact a very charming vision of youth, who proved to me also during my temporary stay extremely sympathetic in character. Of middle stature, attractive rather than pretty, brown ringlets framed her delicate face, out of which roguish eyes peeped above a little snub of a nose; she had a small mouth which showed a row of pearly teeth whenever she spoke or laughed.

" Notwithstanding her gayety, already she had been forced to learn the bitter seriousness of life. Married early to a Frenchman, she passed the first year of her marriage in Paris; but too soon the butterfly husband who was squandering his fortune in frivolity became weary of the little German wife. To get rid of his wife he devised the following scheme : He demanded of her that she should accompany him on a business trip to England; and when they had reached

* For two poems addressed to " Mouche " see vol. iii. pp. 267 and 304. For other verses probably addressed to her, vol. iii. pp. 281 and 282.—TR.

London, he begged her to visit in his company the family of a friend. The carriage stopped in front of a pretty villa, where an old gentleman received her in the most friendly way, and hardly had they been led into an elegant drawing room when her husband disappeared.

" She soon perceived that she was in an insane asylum, and at her screams and tears and prayers to let her go she was threatened with violence in case she did not become quiet. Terror affected the wretched woman to such a degree that she had a paralysis of the tongue which prevented her from speaking for a long time. It was not for several weeks that she became master of herself physically and was able to persuade the physician that she was not mentally ill, upon which her return to Paris was permitted. Further cohabitation with her husband was impossible, and so she gave German lessons in order to assure her own existence.

" Mouche came daily for a few hours to see my brother, and his admiration for the lively little woman unfortunately roused in Mathilde a degree of jealousy amounting to disease, which at last degenerated into animosity. Her husband's

desire that Mouche should be allowed now and
then to share the midday meal was abruptly
refused by Mathilde; Mouche's pleasant greeting
was scarcely returned, and at her appearance the
sick chamber was at once deserted by Mathilde.

"Indeed I was on one occasion mistaken for
Mouche when old Béranger was visiting my
brother. He found me sitting in the twilight
near the bed and, stepping forward, he remarked: 'My dear Heine, is madame the celebrated new reader, Mouche?' To which my
brother answered, laughing: '*Cher ami*, you have
evidently a case of *mouche volante* (trouble of the
eyes). It is my sister.'

"I heard last in 1887, from dear Mouche [Mrs.
Camille Selden], when she informed me that she
had published note-worthy recollections of my
brother and was established in Rouen as teacher
of German at a boarding school for girls.

"My.brother was a great lover of children and
was pleased if the three charming little ones of a
friend of Mathilde, the wife of the director of the
circus, made her a visit; the youngest was his
little godchild. The children were given cookies
and my brother told them lovely fairy stories

which they listened to quietly. On a visit of the
kind, when the glories of heaven were being
recited, as how cookies were to be eaten there
from morning till night, and how the little angels, when they had dined, wiped their mouths
with their white wings instead of a napkin, the
little godchild cried indignantly: 'That is very
dirty of the little angels!' At the same time
I may remark, in contradiction of other statements, that Heine never had an adopted child
—as it has been of late averred.

"At the beginning of December I had news
of the sudden illness of one of my children, and
for that reason resolved to return to Hamburg.
Before going I asked Dr. Gruby what he thought
of my brother's condition; to which I received
the tranquilizing assurance that he might live
from two to three years longer if no unexpected
occurrence intervened. I told my brother of my
near departure and made a solemn promise to
come back in spring. Sorrowfully he received
the news, and begged me, if it were in any way
possible, to return accompanied by my son Ludwig, to whom in his will he had assigned the ex-
ecution of his literary remains, and with whom

he wished to have a personal talk on many points reaching back in the past. At the same time he made extensive explanations to me concerning the disposal of his literary remains, and begged me above all to watch Campe, who was authorized to leave out of the complete works whatever he wished, but was not to add anything of his own motion.

"In order to make my departure easier my brother wrote a lively poem the day before which depicted in amusing fashion my meeting with the family. On the morning of my departure, when I thought to take it from my writing desk where I had laid it down, it was gone, and to my sorrow I learned that the maid-servant had used it to light a fire. When I complained of this to my brother, he said : 'Be comforted, dear sister; when you come back I will write a letter which shall be much more fiery !'

"But there was no coming back for me while he lived, for hardly two months later he entered unexpectedly into eternal rest, and my good-by kiss was the last which I was able to press upon his pale cheek."

A few weeks after the departure of his sister

the condition of Heine grew worse; difficulty of breathing and cramps of the chest became more frequent, often compelling him to pass whole nights in a sitting position in bed. Sleeplessness produced great weakness; but notwithstanding this the poet worked every day for two or three hours. Cramp-like vomitings, which were not to be repressed, began three days before his death, and Dr. Gruby's orders to keep ice bandages on his stomach were able to effect only passing relief. The last night was extremely painful, his weakness grew worse, and the death pangs set in.*

Up to the last moment Heine kept entire consciousness, and died toward five o'clock in the morning on the seventeenth of February 1856.

The funeral took place the twentieth of February on a foggy, cold winter morning at eleven o'clock, and in accordance with the wish expressed in his will to be buried quietly and without ceremonies in the cemetery of Montmartre.†

* See Appendix for the letter of the nurse Catherine Bourlois to Heine's sister.

† See Appendix for the complete legal will, after the original. The German edition gives the French, not a translation into German. In this edition the will is given in English translated from the French.—TR.

The news of the death fell upon his sister with crushing effect; when she left her brother a little while before she had not believed that the day of deliverance from his sufferings could arrive so soon, and the sorrow of his old mother who survived him makes description pointless. The loss of her favorite and the pride of her life threw her on her sick bed; but her powerful constitution won the battle, and it was not till three years later that she slept her last sleep, on the third of September 1859; she and her faithful companion died on the same day of the cholera, which was then raging in Hamburg in the most frightful way.

Scarcely had the earth been packed on Heine's grave when a profitless open quarrel broke out between his brother Gustav and Mathilde as to which had the right to raise a monument to the poet.

Concerning this matter, I had from Mme. Mathilde's side an exhaustive document, which will be found in the Appendix; for the rest I limit myself to the publication of few of her letters, because they were neither composed nor written by her, and merely contain the signature *Veuve Henri Heine* written in her own hand.

Another letter from Mathilde informed me that she did not intend to carry out the third article of my uncle's will.*

This article reads: "I desire that after my death all my papers and my entire correspondence, carefully sealed, shall be kept for the action of my nephew Ludwig von Embden, to whom I shall impart my further intentions concerning them as to the use which he shall make of them, without prejudice to the proprietary rights of my general legatee."

Mme. Mathilde based her refusal to hand the papers over to me on the ground that in the past summer my uncle had wanted to make another will and that she had classified and examined the papers left behind without having discovered the written instructions which I demanded. These statements are to be traced to the counsels of Mme. Mathilde's lawyer, a certain Mr. Julia, and contradict the information

---

* Letters from Mme. Mathilde Heine in the Appendix. (Translated in this edition; the original French in the German edition.)

given by my mother, who had canvassed this matter at length with her brother two months before his death.

Mr. Julia exercised an unlimited influence on Mme. Mathilde and although no document from Heinrich Heine justified it, and his ignorance of the German language did not make him competent so to do, tried to usurp my rights under the will. My feelings rejected a lawsuit directed against Mme. Mathilde, since I had sworn to my uncle always to grant his wife protection and assistance, and I limited my action to urging the fulfillment of the testamentary orders in the most friendly fashion. But my efforts only had effect when Mme. Mathilde had completely thrown Mr. Julia over for reasons which must be kept from publication and which prepared a lamentable close to his unauthorized interference.

Mme. Mathilde placed all the papers left behind at my command with the exception of a fragmentary memoir* which I was not to receive

* For this amusing fragmentary memoir, see vol. v. p. 263. Six pages were destroyed by Max Heine, whose pride seems to have been shoeked by his brother's allusions to family skeletons. See page 316.—Tr,

until after her death, and which she would not permit out of her own hands, because she had been advised to threaten the family with its publication in case her pension were ever withdrawn.

After a careful examination of all the papers left behind, I had the unpublished manuscripts sent to my house in Hamburg, leaving in Paris those of less importance. There remained in Paris, carefully packed up, beside these fragments of a memoir, several packages of odds and ends of manuscripts already published and the letters addressed to Heinrich Heine, the overwhelming majority of which consisted of the business correspondence with Julius Campe.

At the time it occurred Mme. Mathilde's death was concealed from us; neither my mother nor myself were notified and we only learned of her burial through the newspapers. I at once empowered my nephew, then domiciled in Paris, to claim the papers of H. Heine left behind, but received answer that it was too late, since everything had been legally put under seal. From a childish fear of death Mme. Mathilde had made no will and had died suddenly of an apoplexy. As heiress at law the widow Mme. Fauvet, an

old cousin of Mathilde, took out papers; her
maiden name was Mirat and she lived in the village
of Vinot.   The inevitable Mr. Julia had caused
himself to be appointed attorney for this lawful
heir, and in her name he seized everything, even
the papers of Heinrich Heine left by me in Paris.

I demanded in the most energetic way from
Mr. Julia, who had settled himself to housekeeping in Mme. Mathilde's abode, the delivery of
the papers; for it could hardly meet with the
purposes of my uncle Henry Heine, the actual
testator, that his papers should go into the possession of strangers.

The correspondence led to no result and I
went to Paris in order to begin a suit against
Mr. Julia.   My lawyer asserted that he could not
undertake an action against Mr. Julia until I had
won a suit in all forms against the heir at law of
the widow Heine, the widowed Mme. Fauvet.
In order not to carry on as a German a wearisome and costly suit in the French courts, I
proposed to the heiress to pay a sum of money
for her supposed rights as heir to the Heine
papers, but stipulated that Mr. Julia must bind
himself by notarial act that all had been given

up which so far as he knew had been found.
The latter clause was the reason why I never
received an offer to buy the papers as Mr. Julia
promised, and why Mr. Julia, who had decidedly
denied to me the existence of a fragmentary
memoir, sold the few pages of which that memoir
consisted to *Die Gartenlaube* and Mr. Julius
Campe for sixteen thousand francs, after a terrible amount of advertising and through the
offices of a Berlin litterateur.

Mr. Julia boasted that he was the heir of
the Heine relics, but concealed the actual fact
how it was that the fragmentary memoir got
into his hands; his statements concerning it
in R. Fleischer's *Deutsche Revue,* as well as in
various German and French periodicals, statements which bore on their faces the stamp of
dull invention, stood in sharp contrast with the
well known official documents hitherto made
public.

In his biography of Heinrich Heine, Strodtmann says that Campe was exposed after the
death of the poet to the most annoying vexations on the part of the Heine family, that the

latter declined to give assistance in the complete
edition of Heine's works, that they withheld
from him the papers left behind, together with
the document therein drawn up for the proper
arrangement of the volumes, and that they asked
a fabulous sum from him, first thirty thousand
and then twelve thousand francs.

In order to establish the facts in this particular, I may remark that as soon as Mr. Campe the
elder urged me to get him the papers, and as
soon as I had obtained the command of them
and offered them to him for fifteen thousand
francs, he bid twelve thousand francs for them
at once. Then I went personally to Paris in
order to recommend the sale to Mme. Mathilde. It should be understood that, according
to my supposition, there was a good deal among
the papers which had been sold before to Campe,
but had been rejected by the censorship and not
published. In any event a lawsuit would not
have failed to occur had I given over the papers
to another publisher, for I knew old Campe
only too well. Upon my return I informed Mr.
Campe that the widowed Mrs. Heine would
accept his offer, whereupon he answered : "It is

now too late. The complete works are now in the press, and I will only give half that sum."

Irritated by this I broke off all negotiations, and after Campe's death sold the papers to his son and successor for ten thousand francs, which sum the widow Heine received intact. In 1869 the papers left behind appeared, excellently edited by Strodtmann, as a supplementary volume to the great complete works; as he informed me, it was of very respectable profit to the publisher.

The complete works which had appeared before (1861–62) were published by the elder Campe without an invitation to any member of the family to aid him and were edited by Strodtmann. The orders of Heine were ignored not to add anything and to leave out whatever might cause hard feeling. The complete edition included much that was not printed before and in any event ought never to have been published, as, for instance, the poems "Schlosslegende," " Die Weber " * and so forth.

In the fourth article of his will Heinrich Heine ordered :

* For " Die Weber," a savage attack on Germany for her slavishness and apathy, see vol. ii. p. 129.—TR.

"If my friend Campe, the publisher of my works, desires to make any alterations in the way and order after which I have arranged my different writings in the prospectus stated, I desire that no obstacles be placed in his way in this regard, since I have always gladly adapted myself to his necessities as a publisher of books. The main point is that not a line shall be thrust into my writings which I have not expressly intended for publication, or which has been printed without the subscription of my full name. An assumed initial is not enough to ascribe to me a given bit of writing which has been published in one journal or another, since the indication of the author by means of initials always depended on the editors-in-chief, who never could deny themselves the habit of undertaking to make changes in the contents or form of an article signed with initials.

"I forbid expressly that under any excuse whatever, any piece of writing whatever by another person, be that writing as short as may be, shall be added on to my works, unless it were a biographical notice from the pen of one of my old friends whom I had expressly intrusted with such work. I am taking for granted that my

desire in this particular will be carried out loyally
in its fullest sense, that is to say, that my works
shall not be used to take a stranger's writing in
tow or to give that writing publicity."

At the breaking down of negotiations for the
papers left behind Campe had offered three
thousand francs for the handing over of the
document made by Heine for the arrangement
of the complete works, but Mathilde Heine declined the offer squarely in the hope that in that
way she would cause him to accept her demand
for the whole.

This refusal may have been the reason why
Campe thenceforward did not consider himself
bound by the foregoing orders of the will, especially as the public urgently called for an edition augmented in all its parts. It must be re-
corded of Adolf Strodtmann, the editor, that he
accomplished this task with skill, but that by too
great zeal in the endeavor to omit nothing from
the complete works he went too far.

In 1864 the differences between Mme. Mathilde
and the French publishers were arranged by
me, differences arising because the former be-

lieved that she had been deprived of some of her
royalties.   I had no misgivings in fulfilling her
wish to exchange her royalty of twenty-five cen-
times per volume for a single payment of capital,
since her annual pension from Carl Heine (five
thousand francs) and that from Julius Campe
(about three thousand four hundred francs) suf-
ficed to assure her a support for the term of her
life.   I sold the royalty rights of Mme. Mathilde
to the Messrs. Lévy Frères for the sum of
17,500 francs, and after my departure from Paris
she was paid that sum in full.

But new quarrels arose when the letters of
Heinrich Heine appeared (1866) in French ; Mme.
Heine believed that she could demand from the
Messrs. Lévy Frères an extra sum, which the
latter refused.*

The lawsuit which followed turned against the
claims of the widow Heine, despite the fact that
the famous lawyer Jules Favre employed his
whole powers of persuasion to defend her claims.

The mistaken notion that there exist unprinted
manuscripts of Heinrich Heine, which has held

* See Appendix for letters of Mathilde Heine—the French
original in the German edition, a translation in this.—Tr.

its own down to the present, was openly met during her lifetime by Mme. Mathilde by the declaration : " that no one in rightful fashion owns any, and whoever does possess any is called upon to make it known." Furthermore the widow of Heinrich Heine declared in 1869 in the contract of sale for the remaining manuscripts with the Messrs. Hoffmann & Campe* "that all the manuscripts in the literary remains of Heinrich Heine are in the hands of Mr. von Embden, that she (Mme. Heine) does not own any other poems or written works with the exception of a fragmentary memoir, which is not to be published for the present, and that she authorizes the Messrs. Hoffman & Campe to attack anybody, whoever it might be, who should publish anything not yet printed."

Strodtmann made the mistake of believing that all the manuscripts which Heine mentioned in his correspondence from 1823 on were in existence, forgetting that much was destroyed in the fire at Hamburg; and later biographies repeat the same thing with a mysterious solemnity, re-

* See Appendix for the contract of sale made with Hoffmann & Campe.

lying on untrustworthy persons without offering any practical grounds for their assertions.

With respect to the memoir I would like to call to mind once more that in 1833 and 1842 a considerable amount of manuscript was lost by conflagrations, and that the poet himself destroyed them in part voluntarily after his reconciliation with Carl Heine. And even before that, in consequence of financial troubles, he had wedged in various bits from the memoirs into different works piece by piece; for instance, into his " Confessions" and the book about Börne. Throughout his life down to his death Heine wrote at his memoirs and cherished the purpose of publishing the parts already issued along with the newly added as a rounded work. A good part of the fragment published in 1884 was destroyed in the most unauthorized way by Heine's brother Max* in 1867, when he visited the Exposition in Paris and when Mme. Mathilde permitted him in a friendly spirit to look it through. Mme. Mathilde was naturally very much excited at this, called me to Paris, and when I demanded of my uncle an explanation

* See vol. v. p. 266.—Tr.

for this act of violence, he answered: "It was necessary for the fame of his brother to destroy the last pages of a memoir written in the heat of fever in order to make the fragmentary memoir left in Mathilde's hands innocuous."

Mme. Mathilde was unfortunately counseled badly only too often, and the remains, before they came into my hands, were offered to the French Government under Napoleon III for sale at thirty thousand francs, which was refused after a little negotiation. The talk, lately revamped, that the memoirs of Heine exist in the secret archives of the Austrian Government may have sprung up at the time from this fact, that Mr. von Friedland, a friend of Heine for many years, persuaded the readily excited Mme. Mathilde to lend him the memoir manuscripts in order to offer them for sale to the Austrian Government through the instrumentality of Prince Metternich. When I came to Paris and to my astonishment heard of it, I caused Mme. Mathilde to demand the fragmentary memoir back in energetic fashion, and after they had made sure of its harmless contents it was returned to her with thanks. There are no manu-

scripts of Heine in the hands of the Austrian
Government except a few pages of writing—
autographs which were graciously accepted by
her Majesty the Empress in 1887 as a great
admirer of Heine, on the occasion of her visit
to my mother in Hamburg.

That exalted lady cherishes an outspoken
partiality for Heinrich Heine based upon the
finest understanding of him, and when the project of a memorial in Düsseldorf, patronized by
her, came to nothing, she raised to the poet a
monument glorious and full of sentiment in her
marble fairy-palace Achilleion on the island of
Corfu, such a monument as could hardly have
been his in the fatherland.*   A stairway of white
marble of more than a hundred steps leads up
from the seashore by the slope of a wooded hill,
and high above on a piece that juts off from the
stair there rises a six-columned temple of white
marble open on all sides, with a rounded roof.
In the center of this graceful building, shaded by
enormous silvery gray olive trees, is the life size
portrait of Heinrich Heine in marble, a creation
of the Danish sculptor Hasselriis, who lives in

* See the cut after a photograph of this statue.—Tʀ.

THE MARBLE STATUE BY HASSELRIIS, ERECTED AT CORFU
BY THE EMPRESS OF AUSTRIA.

Rome. The serious statue, full of sentiment,
looks out on that sea which the poet has sung
so truly and with such touching beauty, and
represents him sitting in the last stage of his incurable sickness, with head hanging forward and
closed eyes from which the tears are oozing.
One hand holds a pencil, the other a piece of
paper with the words of the song:

> Whence, with a blur of vision,
> Com'st thou, O lonely tear?
> Mine eyes have kept thee hidden
> This many a long past year.

Mme. Mathilde lived for a long period in
an unpretending, very comfortable dwelling *aux
Batignolles rue l'Ecluse*, the back of which permitted of a view upon gardens full of flowers.
In that house there ruled the most perfect order
and cleanliness, to which the industrious Pauline
attended with never a break. Mme. Mathilde's
recreations consisted of a visit to the circus or
the little theater on the boulevard when amusing
pieces were played there, or else of a walk with
Pauline to the Champs Elysées.* Besides this
a weighty rôle was played in her case by the

---

[1] For Heine's forecast of his wife's behavior after his death, see
the amusing verses "Gedächtnissfeier," vol. iii. p. 118.—TR,

pleasures of the table, and if I was her guest she had the favorite dish of her *pauvre Henri* prepared and in accordance with her childlike character thought in that way to honor his memory very specially. It was touching with what pious affection she talked about him and confided to me that people had often asked for her hand in marriage, but that she could never make up her mind to forget her Henri and lay aside his famous name.

When her *pauvre Henri* was very angry indeed because she had spent too much money, or sorrowfully thought about his mother and sister in Germany, a single caress had ever been sufficient to turn his mood to gayety and gladness.

> Here comes, as lovely as the dawn to-morrow,
> My wife, and smiles away my German sorrow !

Mathilde was a great lover of animals ; besides Cocotte she had an aviary with fifty or sixty canaries, and three white Bologna dogs. When the whole menagerie began to scream, twitter and bark the noise was unbearable, and when I made as if to run away in a hurry, she would say in a surprised tone: *C'est drôle ; vous êtes comme vôtre oncle, qui n'aimait pas les bêtes.*

During the siege Mathilde remained in Paris, and later complained to me of what she had to stand during that time; she had to give two hundred francs for a chicken. Then when I expressed my astonishment that she could have paid such a price, she would answer, smiling: *Que faire, si c'etait le prix?* She never learned to value the worth of money and always remained the big, harmless child she had been! She generally passed the summer months in the country, and about two years before her death I visited her for the last time in Longjumeau, where she was then staying; it was in an airy, roomy dwelling and she showed me with childlike joy the fruit trees and shady arbors in the big garden.

Since my last meeting with her Mathilde's exterior had greatly changed; her hair had whitened, her corpulency had increased in a frightful degree, and complaints of rheumatic troubles fell from the mouth which formerly only laughed. After a copious breakfast the usual pleasant mood returned to her once more, and after a few hours of happy conference when she embraced me for good-by she little imagined that there would be no further meeting between us.

On the seventeenth of February 1883, on the day that her husband died, Mathilde stood at the window of her house in Passy, and though but a little before she had been talking with Pauline, fell suddenly to the floor dead, struck by an apoplexy.

After twenty-seven years the grave reunited her once more with her beloved husband, whose life she had brightened with her loveliness and gay spirits and whose heavy sufferings during so many hours she had driven from his mind!

May the publication of the foregoing family letters of Heinrich Heine, knit together with a brief glance at his earlier life, serve as a guard against further misleading statements concerning the poet, as well as concerning his relations to his family! and at the same time may it serve the dead as a permanent work of reminiscence and of admiration.

We may fairly suit his own words to these letters :

> All my torture and lamentings,
>   Lo, within this book I pour you,
> And when you have raised the cover
>   Open lies my heart before you.

APPENDIX.

APPENDIX.

I

LETTER FROM THE NURSE CATHERINE BOUR-
LOIS TO MRS. CHARLOTTE EMBDEN IN HAM-
BURG.

(*Translated from the French.*)

PARIS, March 11, 1858.

MADAME:

I have just sent to your honored brother very
long details which he asked for concerning
the death of Mr. Heine. Mme. Mathilde, your
sister-in-law, left the house of the dead one hour
and a half before the interment; she has not yet
returned to the house on Avenue Montaigne,
but Miss Pauline comes every day to get her letters from the janitor. I do not know Mme.
Heine's address.

The day preceding his death my poor master said: "I am glad my family has come, for I

shall never see them more." He regretted very
much not to have written on Wednesday, because later he was no longer able to.   During the
last night he kept repeating, as he had repeated
on Friday : " I am done for!" during that
fatal night I had a watcher with me and I went
to wake Miss Pauline when I saw the end approaching I could have easily called Madame,but
the least noise might have made his last moments
more painful, and I feared the effect that the
death of a husband ought to produce on his
wife, nevertheless Miss Pauline ran to Madame's
room just before the final moment, and I only
had time to tell her on the threshold of the
door : " All is over!"

A quarter of an hour before dying, Mr. Heine
had complete consciousness.   I encouraged him
and consoled him as well as I could every
moment, but he saw as we did that the medi-
cines produced no relief whatever.   The attachment he had for you and the demand you
made on me when leaving made it my duty to
write to you ; I have done so without notifying
Mme. Heine, will you therefore please, Madame,
avoid speaking to her of my letters? and if you

have new commands to lay on me, please add to my address: *Commune de Passy, Rue du bel air, barrière de l'Etoile, Paris.*

Not having been correctly addressed, your letter did not arrive till the 9th.

I am, Madame, your very humble servant,
CATHERINE BOURLOIS.

I should add that on Saturday at four or five in the afternoon Master called me three times in succession he told me to write . . . but not understanding the meaning of his words and not wishing to force him to repeat them, I answered Yes. I said to him a little later: when your vomiting ceases you must write yourself ; he answered, I am going to die.

II

WILL OF HEINRICH HEINE.

(Translated from the French.)

Before Mr. Ferdinand Léon Ducloux and Mr.
Charles Emile Rousse, notaries of Paris subscribing,

And in the presence of :

1. Mr. Michel Jacob, merchant baker, living in
Paris at No. 60 Rue d'Amsterdam,
2. And Mr. Eugène Grouchy, merchant grocer,
living in Paris at No. 52 Rue d'Amsterdam,

Both the witnesses being clothed with the
conditions demanded by law according as they
have made declaration to the notaries subscribed
in the examination which has been made of each
of them separately,

And in the bedchamber of Mr. Heine, herein-
after mentioned, situate on the second story of
No. 50, a house on the Rue d'Amsterdam, in
which bedchamber, lighted by a window on the
courtyard, the notaries and the witnesses chosen

by the testator came together at the express demand of the latter

Appeared

Mr. Henri Heine, man of letters and doctor of laws, living in Paris at No. 50 Rue d'Amsterdam.

The same being sick of body, but well in mind, memory and hearing, according as it appeared to the said notaries and witnesses after conversing with him, has, in consideration of his death, dictate, to the said Mr. Ducloux, in presence of Mr. Rousse and the witnesses, his will and testament in the following manner :

§ 1. I constitute for my universal legatee Mme. Mathilde Crescense Heine, born Mirat, my legal spouse, with whom for many long years I have passed my good seasons and bad, and who has cared for me during the long and cruel continuance of my malady. I leave to her in full and complete ownership, and without any conditions or restrictions, everything that I possess and that I may possess at my death, and all my rights and dues under any form soever.

§ 2. At a time when I looked forward to a wealthy future, I parted with all my literary property on very modest terms ; unfortunate

events have the rather swallowed up the little
means I owned and my disease does not allow
me to relieve my fortunes a little for the benefit
of my wife. The pension which I enjoy from
my uncle, the late Salomon Heine, and which
was always the foundation of my estimate of
income, has been assured to my wife in part only.
I myself desired that it should be so. At the
present moment I feel the greatest regret at
having failed to arrange better for the comfort
of my wife after my death. The said pension
from my uncle represented in the beginning the
interest on a sum of money which that paternal
benefactor did not care to place in the hands of
one like myself, a poet unused to business, in
order to assure to me a lasting enjoyment
thereof. I was counting on that annuity when
I joined to my own lot a person whom my uncle
honored greatly and to whom he gave many a
sign of affection—though he has done nothing
for her of an official sort in the arrangements for
his will. It is no less to be presumed that this
forgetfulness was due to a fatal chance rather
than the sentiments of the deceased. He whose
generosity has enriched and dowered so many

persons who are strangers to his family and his
heart cannot be accused of a shabby stinginess
when the matter at issue was the lot of the wife
of a nephew who has made his name glorious.
The slightest gestures and words of a man who
was generosity itself ought to be interpreted as
generous. A son worthy of his father, my
cousin Charles Heine has agreed with me in
these opinions, and with a noble eagerness he
acceded to my request when I begged him to
take a formal engagement to pay to my wife
after my death, as an annuity, one-half of the
yearly pension which dated from his late
father; that stipulation was entered into the
twenty-fifth of February 1847; and I am still
agitated at memory of the noble reproaches
which, notwithstanding our differences of that
period, my cousin made me on the score of my
lack of confidence in his feelings with regard to
my wife. When he offered me his hand as a
guarantee of his promise, I pressed it against my
poor, sick eyes and bedewed it with my tears.
Since then my position has grown worse and my
illness has put an end to many of the sources of
income which I might have left to my wife;

these unexpected vicissitudes and other grave
causes compel me to apply again to the worthy and
rightful feelings of my cousin ; I beseech him not
to lessen my said pension by one-half, but continue
it to my wife after my death, and to pay it to her
in full just as I received it during my uncle's life.

I say intentionally "just as I received it during
my uncle's life," because for almost five years,
since my illness has increased in seriousness, my
cousin, Charles Heine, has more than doubled the
amount of my pension, a generous attention for
which I cherish for him a great gratitude.   It is
more than likely that I shall not need to make
this appeal to the liberality of my cousin, because
I am certain that with the first bit of earth which
he shall toss upon my tomb, according to his
right as my nearest of kin, if he should be in Paris
at the time of my death, he will forget all the
wretched grievances which I have so greatly regretted and expiated by a long agony.   Surely
he will then remember the great friendship of
long ago, the affinity and similarity of feelings
which united us from the time of our tender
youth; and he will vow an entirely fraternal sentiment of protection for the widow of his friend ;

but it is not useless for the quiet of all concerned that the living should know what it is that the dead ask at their hands.

§ 3. I desire that after my death all my papers and all my letters shall be scrupulously locked up and held at the command of my nephew Ludwig von Embden, to whom I shall give my final instructions as to the use he shall make of them, without prejudice to the proprietary rights of my universal legatee.

§ 4. If I die before the complete edition of my works shall have appeared and I shall not have been able to preside at the management of that edition, or if my death shall have taken place before it is finished, I beg my relative Dr. Rudolph Christiani to take my place in the management of said publication while confining himself strictly to the prospectus which I shall have left for that purpose. If my friend Mr. Campe, the editor of my works, desires to make any changes in the method whereby I have ordered my various writings in the said prospectus, I desire that no difficulties be placed in his way in this respect, seeing that I have always been glad to accommodate myself to his necessities as a publisher. The main thing is that there shall not be intercalated in my writings any line which I did not expressly design for publicity or which has been printed without the signature of my name in full. A conventional initial is not enough to attribute to me a writing published by some paper, seeing that the indication of an author by initials always depended on the editors-in-chief, who moreover have never forbidden themselves the custom of making radical changes or alterations in form in an article signed only by initials; I expressly forbid that under any pretext any writing by another, let it be as insignificant as it may, shall be fastened on to my works, unless it should be a biographical notice coming from the pen of one of my old friends to whom I have made an express demand for such a task. I expect that in this respect, that is to say, that my works shall not be used to take in tow, nor to propagate, any alien work, my desires shall be loyally carried out in all their length and breadth.

§ 5. I forbid that my body after death shall be submitted to an autopsy; only as my illness often resembles a case of catalepsy I think that the precaution should be taken to open a vein before my burial.

§ 6. If I am in Paris at the time of my death and am dwelling not too far away from Montmartre, I desire to be buried in the cemetery so named, since I have a predilection for that quarter, where I resided for many years.

§ 7. I ask that my burial procession shall be as modest as possible, and that the cost of my burial shall not exceed the ordinary amount for that of the simplest citizen. Although I belong by virtue of baptism to the Lutheran confession, I do not wish that the clergy of that Church shall be summoned to my burial; I decline the ministration indeed of every other priesthood for the celebration of my obsequies; this wish is not dictated by any feeble boast of a freethinker's position. For four years past I have abdicated every sort of philosophical pride and have returned to religious ideas and feelings. I die believing in the One and Eternal God, Creator of the world, whose mercy I beseech for my immortal soul. I regret having sometimes spoken in my writings of Sacred Things without the reverence which is their due, but I was drawn aside

rather by the spirit of my epoch than by my individual leaning. If, unknown to me, I have
offended against righteous custom and morality,
which is the true essence of all monotheistic
beliefs, I ask pardon therefor of God and mankind.* I forbid that any discourse, either in German or French, shall be held at my grave. At
the same time I state the wish, however happy
the lot of our country shall become, that my
compatriots shall abstain from transferring my
ashes to Germany; I have never liked to lend my
person to political mummeries. The grand business of my life has been to labor for a cordial
understanding between Germany and France,
and to defeat the strategems of the enemies
of democracy, who for their own gain exploit
international prejudices and animosities. I believe that I have done well by my compatriots
as by the French people also, and the titles
to their gratitude which I have earned are un-
doubtedly the most precious legacy which I have
to leave to my universal legatee.

§ 8. I nominate as executor of my will Mr.
Maxime Joubert, counselor at the Court of Ap-

* For Heine's Apology see vol. xii. p. 194.—TR.

peals, and I thank him for being so good as to take the charge of this office.

The above will was dictated in these terms by Mr. Henri Heine and written in its entirety by the hand of Mr. Ducloux, one of the subscribing notaries, just as it was dictated to him by the testator, all in presence of the said notaries and witnesses, the same, being questioned on that matter, having declared that they were not the relatives of the legatee.

And the same being read to the testator in the presence of the same persons, the testator declared that it contained the expression of his wishes.

Made and concluded at Paris in the bed-chamber of Mr. Heine here below inscribed.

Year 1851, Thursday, thirteenth of November, about six o'clock in the afternoon.

And after a re-reading from beginning to end, the testator and witnesses have signed along with the notaries.

Registered at Paris in Third Bureau
the twentieth of February 1856,

III

LETTERS FROM MRS. MATHILDE HEINE, WIDOW.

(Translated from the French.)

PARIS, March 25, 1856.

MY DEAR NEPHEW:

I received your two letters, and thank you for the kind words which they contain. Your father also honored me by sending me a touching letter which has given me great pleasure. Be kind enough to tell him, I beg you, that for a long while I have cherished for him a great esteem, and that I make it a duty in the present instance to send him, with my most lively thanks, an assurance of my most affectionately distinguished sentiments.

I did hope, this I confess, to find the same actions on the part of all the members of my husband's family; my hopes in this respect have not been fulfilled. Doubtless you have not been without news of the very serious offense which I have received from my brother-in-law, Mr. Gus-

338

tave Heine of Vienna. He was not content with giving no sign of life in my regard, although I had begged Dr. Gruby, my husband's physician, to announce to him the death of his brother, as to the other members of the family. After having abandoned me to my own resources in the accomplishment of the first and indispensable duties, those which are effected without noise and such as are not put in the newspapers, with the result that I was obliged to have recourse to strangers, he caused to be published in a German paper and reproduced in the French journals, the following note:

" Mr. Gustave Heine, brother of the famous Henri Heine, who died recently in Paris, will raise a monument to his brother at a cost of ten thousand francs. Mr. Gustave Heine, who lives in Vienna, has had the design of the monument made here; it was forwarded to Paris yesterday."

This paragraph was in itself an offense quite serious enough ; for after all, without having announced it to me, a notification was given to the public of a purpose which affected me more than any other person, and one to which Mr. Gustave

Heine could only give effect with my own consent.

And indeed at first I considered this paragraph to be one of those rumors which newspapers circulate, and which have nothing exact in them. What caused me to think that was, not alone my own rights ignored and propriety trampled under foot, but also, and particularly, the cost of the monument so proudly placarded in a newspaper article. I could not imagine that my brother-in-law, in a matter so sad and in connection with an act so elevated in character, so sacred, so veritably religious, would wish to put himself in the way of appearing to yield to a motive purely ostentatious. My first care, therefore, was to answer this paragraph with the following letter:

"PARIS, March 10, 1856.

"DEAR SIR:

"I learn that you have reproduced the paragraph issued by the *Augsburg Gazette* relating to an alleged monument which Mr. Gustave Heine of Vienna was proposing to erect to the memory of the late Henri Heine, my husband.

"Permit me to state here, sir, that I have bought

in the cemetery of Montmartre a lot of land in
order to establish there the perpetual sepulcher
of my husband, and that no one may undertake
to raise a monument there without having made
a preliminary arrangement with me. Up to this
moment having received no notification of the
proceeding mentioned by the *Augsburg Gazette,*
it is certainly allowable for me to add that this
action, to which the German papers have given
some circulation, should be for the present considered by the public of no effect.

" I have the honor etc.,

" (signed) WIDOW HENRI HEINE."

After he read that letter Mr. Gustave Heine
might have repaired everything; he ought to
have tried. He ought to have written to the
papers to say that in fact he did have the intention of raising a monument to the memory of
his brother but he meant to act in no wise outside me and without me. Far from that, he has
addressed the following letter to the *Journal
des Débats :*

" SIR:

" The papers have announced that I have
the intention of causing a monument to be
erected to the memory of my brother Henri
Heine and that the designs for said monument
have been sent on to Paris to be carried out.

" In my quality of elder brother of the deceased
and at the expressed wish of my venerable
mother I shall fulfill the sacred duty to mark for
posterity in a worthy fashion the place where
those famous remains, dear to my affection, lie
buried. To that end I have commissioned two
celebrated artists of Vienna to compose two
different designs for monuments in marble and
granite ; but before having them carried out,
moved by a feeling of filial piety, I have considered it my duty to send the designs in question
to Hamburg in order to obtain the advice of my
mother and to regulate accordingly my final choice.

" GUSTAVE HEINE,

"*Editor-in-Chief of the Fremdenblatt.*

" VIENNA, March 14, 1856."

This time, while having the air of trampling all
my rights under foot, while speaking as if I had

no existence or as if I had deserved that the family of my husband should put me to one side in so important a matter, Mr. Gustave Heine himself has done me a very grave injury. I therefore have been forced to come to a decision. That decision is that no one save myself shall continue to take charge of the beloved and sacred remains of my poor husband. Consequently I have answered the *Journal des Débats :*

"PARIS, March 21, 1856.

" SIR :

" In my letter of the tenth of this month which you have had the kindness to publish I had the honor of letting you know that, having bought a piece of land in order to establish on it the perpetual sepulcher of Henri Heine, my husband, no person has the right to elevate a mausoleum on that grave without my consent.

" To-day, after the appearance of the letter from Vienna which you inserted in your number of day before yesterday, I consider that I ought to go further, and I declare that I shall permit no one to share with me in the care to arrange a

APPENDIX.

final and pious abode for a man of genius who
did me the honor of associating his life with
mine and who besides kept for me down to his
last day his finest and his most affectionate regards.

"Accept, etc.,

WIDOW HENRI HEINE."

At any rate I have had the consolation of find-
ing here among the newspapers the most lively
and complete sympathy. I have seen no one who
has not seemed indignant that anyone should
profit by a moment when I had just been overwhelmed by a frightful disaster in order to make
me suffer through attempts at persecution. People were particularly astonished at the fact that the
act emanated from my brother-in-law and was directed against a woman. People knew the way
in which my husband adored me, and considered
evil acts aimed at his widow in the light of an
outrage to his memory. There was nothing in
the letter of my brother-in-law, even to the part
relating to my mother-in-law, which did not give
occasion for the severest blame. People generally found that it in no wise lessened the insult

which he gave me to put it under the cloak of
the worthy desires of my venerated mother-in-
law, whom I learned from my husband to esteem
and love. Finally, some people went so far as to
say that the purpose of my brother-in-law was
simply a desire to call attention to himself and
in no respect to do what he announced. They
furnish proof for this reasoning by saying that
the man who desires to carry a thing to comple-
tion does not voluntarily place himself in the ab-
solute impossibility of accomplishing it, by doing
outrage without any sort of necessity to the only
person who has the power to grant him the right.

As to myself, my dear nephew, I have allowed
all this to be said without aiding it with my own
reflections. Plunged in grief, living in retirement, I have only left for a moment and to my
great regret the profound silence which I have
imposed upon myself in order to defend my
dignity and my ignored rights. I was absolutely
bound to do so, not merely with regard to
myself, but also with regard to my poor husband,
to whose wishes and to whose memory I would
think myself but little faithful if I permitted
anyone, whoever he might be, under whatsoever

pretext, to aim a blow at the rights which I hold
through his act, and should I degrade in my person the dignity of the individual whom he has
loved the most.

Accept, my dear nephew, etc.,

WIDOW HENRI HEINE.

PARIS, March, 1856.

MY DEAR NEPHEW:

In special answer to your letter you seem astonished because Mr. Joubert has not written
to you and because I have not myself sent you
the papers and the few remaining letters which
my husband had preserved. Allow me to observe
to you that the honorable Mr. Joubert had no
reason to write; he was merely to send you a
copy of the will if one was asked from him, and
that is what he did. Moreover he was waiting
for you to send him, or for you to forward to me
in person the instructions which my husband
wished to send you when he made his will,
instructions without which the orders which he
gives you are entirely impossible to carry out
and in consequence become of no effect, now it
appears from your letter that you have not

received those instructions. you therefore beg me to send them to you, believing in error that I have them. I have nothing of the kind and have never had them, nay more, while classifying my husband's papers I went over them one by one and found nothing which resembled instructions. After all, that does not surprise me. I knew that my husband had changed his mind after his will, especially since last summer; he had decided to leave to me myself the liberty of disposing of all manuscripts as I thought fit. He told me that very often, and it is proved moreover by a will which he had begun a few days before dying and which death, alas! interrupted. In that draft, written with his own hand, my poor husband is not content with instituting me once more his universal legatee without condition or restriction; he goes so far as to give me, by the public homage which he renders me, a fresh mark of that lofty esteem and that steady and unchangeable sympathy which united us so closely for so long a term of years. It is a sweet consolation and a very lively happiness for my heart to think that up to his last moment I was the most active and almost sole preoccupation of a great man and of a great man whom I loved.

There only remains for me, dear nephew, to express well to you the feelings of gratitude with which I am filled when thinking over the words of devotion and love which your letter contains. Be well assured that I in my turn remember with pleasure my nephew Ludwig, and that I hope to hear good news from him whenever the occasion serves.

Accept, I pray you, my dear nephew, and be so good as to offer to all Your family assurances of my most distinguished sentiments.

WIDOW HENRI HEINE.

PARIS, February 20, 1867.

To Mr. Jules Claretie,

SIR: *The Figaro.*

How do you know of the lawsuit which I have begun against Mr. Michel Lévy? I live in great retirement and make no noise concerning the sentiment which has impelled me to avenge the memory of my husband hatefully outraged.

So it is my adversary who has plead his case

before you, and his arguments—with none to answer—have caused you to write these words:

" I am fain to believe that Mme. Heine, perceiving that she has been ill counseled, will not push the matter farther. . . "

You are mistaken, sir—in a suit of this kind counselors are only of use to point out my path; I act spontaneously, strong in my own conscience, not for a matter of money, but for a question of honor. For your personal instruction here are the facts:

Men of letters, I have often heard it said, are little boys in business matters in comparison with Messieurs the publishers. Consider then my inexperience as a mere woman when I negotiated with Mr. Michel Lévy!

But he was so kind, so thoughtful that I did not dream of being on my guard. One day, touched by his solicitude, I told him that people were publishing my husband's letters in foreign parts, letters pretending to be private but rather fabricated. I was sorrowful enough; but how can one enter suit in Germany! Get those books for me, answered Mr. Lévy, and I will go and ask one hundred thousand francs of damages from the publisher for you.

I mention these figures in order to be the more exact : I only wanted one thing, to stop the publication, and I had the good luck to meet a protector in order to reach my ends! Having made inquiry I bought seven volumes in German which I gave to him.

Months, years passed.   I asked Mr. Michel Lévy for the books which I had intrusted to him, since he did nothing in defense of my rights, but he was always so much occupied and the pamphlets were so far off on the shelves that I had patience and waited still longer, when I heard very indirectly that Mr. Michel Lévy was pub-lishing these letters, fabricated and translated, which excited his anger at an earlier period. Whence a suit, and without saying anything bad of the judges in Berlin, I shall find my judges this time in Paris : the aim seems to me less diffi-cult of attainment.

Do you know of these facts, sir ?   I am sure in advance that you do not, and nevertheless they are mentioned in my summons.

You shall no longer have the right to laugh at

me. In your turn you played the game of Mr. Michel Lévy. You thought he was relating to you a singular suit, and he only desired ten lines in your newspaper, knowing well that, written by you, they would be a recommendation which would cause a quantity of books to be sold for him before the verdict of the court. I beg you, sir, to insert this letter in your next number. I do not speak to you of my rights: it is a prayer I address to you with an expression of my best sentiments.

WIDOW HENRI HEINE.

IV

To Mr. Jules Claretie,
      Editor of the Figaro.

SIR :

The reflections which the lawsuit instituted against us by Mme. Widow Heine has inspired in you, with respect to the Correspondence of her husband, the first two volumes of which we recently published, have brought forth a pretended rectification signed by that lady; she accuses you of having made yourself my complaisant advocate with an aim at a mercantile advertisement.

In so far as touches the accusation of complaisance, you know, sir, how gratuitous the supposition of Mme. Heine is, and whether I have the honor of knowing you sufficiently to be justified in asking a service from you.

As to the grounds of debate it is not in a newspaper that it is proper to consider them in detail. This is what I shall confine myself to saying for sole justification. Article I. of the contract which I concluded with Mme. Heine the twenty-eighth of January 1865 reads as follows:

" 1. The full and entire ownership of all the works of Henri Heine appeared or still to appear.

" 2. The exclusive right of translation into French of all the works of Henri Heine published in the German language.

" 3. The right of translation into French of all the works of Henri Heine, posthumous and unpublished, which have just appeared."

By virtue of the rights which this article intrusts so explicitly to me, I caused to be translated the "Correspondence of Henri Heine," which forms the volumes xix, xx, and xxi, of the original edition of the complete works of Henri Heine, published at Hamburg by Hoffmann & Campe, grantees from Mme. Widow Heine by the same right as myself and the German publishers of her husband for more than forty years, just as I am myself his French publisher since about fourteen years. This origin of my translation is a concrete fact, easy to corroborate, and one which apparently Mme. Heine or rather the persons who advise her have not taken the trouble to verify, but one which the wisdom of the bench will not fail to examine into.

An unauthorized edition of certain works of Henri Heine was published in seven volumes at Amsterdam by Binger Brothers. This edition was in truth called to my attention by Mme. Heine two or three years ago, who placed in my hands a copy as a document to produce, in case I judged it proper to attack the publishers at law. But I have borrowed absolutely nothing from that edition, I never caused a single line to be translated, and this I should have proved to Mme. Heine if she, before sending me a summons, had been so kind as to come and see me, as perhaps my pleasant relations with her might have urged her to do.

I still hope that, convinced of my good faith from the palpable proofs with which I confront her, Mme. Heine will withdraw the complaint which certain awkward givers of advice have caused her to enter so lightly against me.

Receive, sir, assurance of my most distinguished consideration.

MICHEL LÉVY.

P. S.—Mme. Heine speaks of her inexperience
and gives to understand that I got the better of
her at the time of the conclusion of our contract.
Now it was not with her personally that I negotiated the matter; it was with Mr. von Embden
of Hamburg, nephew and friend of Henri Heine,
whom she had intrusted with her interests and
who came to Paris expressly to reach an understanding with me. Mme. Heine only had the
trouble of placing her signature at the foot of
the contract, just as doubtless happened with the
letters which she wrote you.

V

CONTRACT WITH MESSRS. HOFFMANN & CAMPE *in re* THE LITERARY REMAINS OF HENRI HEINE.

(*Translated from the French.*)

1. For the sum of ten thousand francs, the posthumous works of Henri Heine, which are at present in the hands of Mr. von Embden.

2. Mme. H. Heine Widow declares that she possesses nothing more in the way of poems or other literary product of H. Heine, except a fragment of memoirs, and (this) she will not publish for the present.

3. She also authorizes Messrs. Hoffmann & Campe to call to account whomsoever it may be who shall publish still other unpublished matter, naturally at the cost and expense of Messrs. Hoffmann & Campe.

HAMBURG, August 16, 1869.